Peter Eickhof

111 places
in Vienna
that you shouldn't
miss

With photographs by Karl Haimel

emons:

Bibliographical information of the Deutsche Nationalbibliothek
The Deutsche Nationalbibliothek lists this publication
in the Deutsche Nationalbibliografie; detailed bibliographical
data are available on the internet at http://dnb.d-nb.de.

© Hermann-Josef Emons Verlag
All rights reserved
© Photographs: Karl Haimel
Design: Eva Kraskes, based on a design
by Lübbeke | Naumann | Thoben
Maps: Frederik von Reumont
English translation: David Andersen
Printing and binding: B.O.S.S Druck und Medien GmbH, Goch
Printed in Germany 2013
ISBN 978-3-95451-206-5
First edition

For the latest information about emons, read our regular newsletter:
order it free of charge at www.emons-verlag.de

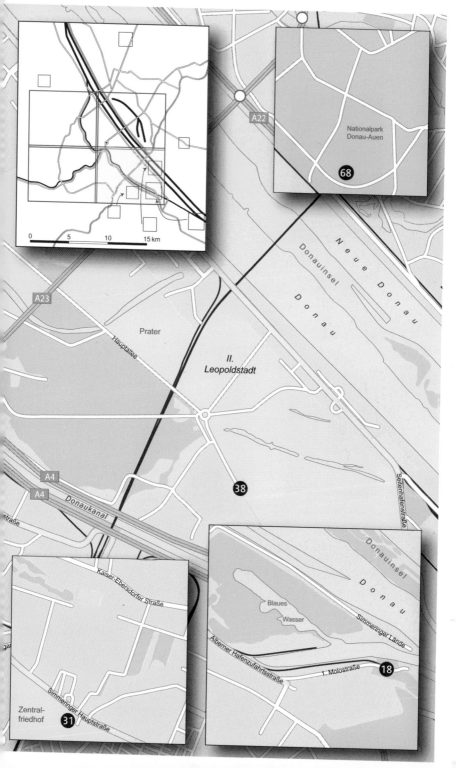

The Author

Peter Eickhoff frequently lives in Vienna. His most recent publications were »111 Orte in Düsseldorf, die man gesehen haben muss« and »111 Orte am Niederrhein, die man gesehen haben muss«.

The Photographer

Karl Haimel was born in the Leopoldstadt, a district of Vienna. After spending time in Germany, Canada, Peru, and Venezuela, he has now returned to Vienna. His photopraphs have been exhibited, among other venues, in Bogotá, Havana, Cracow, Lima, Helsinki, Moscow, and Prag.

Foreword

In Vienna even the usual sights are worth seeing, so it isn't a mistake to follow the fixed stars, the perfectly restored and constantly re-painted great historical and architectural attractions that, as the brightly-lit, atmospheric backdrop, decorate the familiar scenes of Vienna. Admittedly, Vienna and its inhabitants are replete with a fabulous repertoire of old images and buildings – and, of course, with stories, which always have a typically vintage Viennese coziness, are altogether critical and sometimes equivocal, brimming with human forbearance, and *schmäh*, the typical Viennese snide humor, and are therefore, on occasion, ruthlessly charming. As always, the city presents itself as an imperial fairytale waltz, glittering like gold – like the statue of Johann Strauss in the municipal park – animated by immortal melodies and sweet pastries, a little bit outside time and yet as outmodedly nostalgic as a horse-drawn *fiaker* carriage ride during rush hour. In Vienna each past has experienced its inexorable present.

But Vienna is writing new stories. Vienna hardly recognizes itself; it is different, just as the city's promotion swears. Vienna's new realities are colorful, sometimes flamboyant, polyglot and multilingual, with a much faster rhythm than the dreamy old waltzes. The city is increasingly insisting that we gladly accept the differences and their life-affirming diversity. As it always has been, Vienna is a city full of epicenters that create a feeling of immediacy. Vienna as an exemplary site of a modern society. You can follow the voices that are telling Vienna's new stories at 111 places – each, without exception, interesting in its own way.

111 Places

1 The Alt Wien

A moveable feast

About the only thing this café has in common with the classic coffeehouse is the coffee. It was established in 1936 as »Kaffee Alt Wien«. Leopold Hawelka, who became Vienna's most famous café owner, and his wife, Frau Josefine, who became something like the Inner City district's midnight dumpling queen, ran it for three short years before they opened the »Hawelka« in Dorotheergasse, which has since become a permanent fixture in Vienna. This scuffed and raggedy institution with the worn-out chairs that warm not only the behinds but also the hearts of old Bohemians is located in the area where tourists head if they are interested in art, and who aim their ever-ready digital cameras at anyone who hasn't shaved in two days.

What »Hawelka« once was in its best years, »Alt Wien« still is. It is loud, full of great plans for the future and neuroses, fast-moving with flashes of brilliance, cynical, jittery, drunken, exhibitionistic, and somehow creative. Commonly recognizable A-list celebrities are not much in evidence, but when they do show up, they usually squelch the feel-good atmosphere. The artists and writers in »Alt Wien« are usually still somewhat young, but Helmut Qualtinger, who was for a time one of the gaped-at tourist attractions in the »Hawelka« (before he sought refuge in the »Alt Wien« and the »Café Gutruf«), knew in his defining role as Herr Karl, »I was also once a younger man.«

And, as we all know, that changes faster than you think. Then, looking back, there is a lot to tell: for example, how great life and partying was back then in the »Alt Wien«. It was always best around midnight in the historic »year of 2012« when everything was still ahead of you that you now look back on wistfully: on the youthful gift of anarchy that you simply had to live out in your early twenties and on the small serving of goulash that was sometimes fantastic, and on the many exhibition and film posters that papered the walls.

Address 1st district, Bäckerstrasse 9 | Transport bus 1a to Riemergasse; bus 2a to Roten-turmstrasse | Opening times daily 10am–2am | Tip Absolutely exquisite organic ice cream is being sold not far away, in Rotenturmstrasse 14, in the recently opened »Eis-Greissler«.

2 The Amalienbad

Red waves

From the outside, it looks like the Favoriten district's whitewashed stronghold of the privileged, rather unapproachable and closed off, as if the baths and its facilities were defending themselves against attacks from a hostile world. The Amalienbad stands in the midst of the particularly dry and stabile pathos of blue-collar architecture characteristic of most of the historical municipal buildings of »Red Vienna«. It isn't until you are in the great swimming pool hall that the optimistic, bright, light-flooded vision is revealed that the working class had of itself in the 1920s. At the time, the working class was engrossed in creating its own anti-bourgeois culture, and so the Amalienbad, which was opened in 1926 with a great public celebration, became a concept of society and life for the working class. Which is why it wasn't named after a god of antiquity or a representative of the House of Habsburg, but rather the seamstress Amalie Pölzer (born a baroness, by the way), who was, at the time, a universally loved women's rights campaigner and a member of the central committee of the Social Democratic Workers' Party of Austria.

It was one of the largest and most modern prestigious building projects of the government of Vienna. Today it is privately run. The original bathhouse, damaged during the war but largely restored to its original condition, was so designed that when competitions took place there, spectator stands could be set up, and the glass roof rolled back. There was a sauna and a steam bath, hairdressing salons, and seemingly downright upper-class wellness studios.

Back then, dashing workers, both male and female, tried to impress others not only by diving head-first from the 10-meter tower, but also by swimming across the pool end-to-end, a 33.3-meter long stretch, not once, but a dozen times. Today, people tend to swim across the pool (12.5 meters) in the historic hall, which, due to a lack of physical condition and set rules, continually leads to polyglot shoving matches and ethnical misunderstandings.

Address 10th district, Reumannplatz 23 | Transport U1, bus 66A, 67A, 70a to Reumann-platz | Opening times Mon 12:30pm –3pm (senior citizens only), Tue 9am–6pm, Wed 9am–9:30pm, Thu 7am–9:30pm, Fri 9am–9:30pm, Sat 7am–8pm, Sun 7am–6pm | Tip Jörgerbad in Hernals, Jörgerstrasse 42–44, Vienna's oldest bathhouse, is not quite as opulent but is preserved in all its beauty.

3_ The Anzengruber

The art of drinking

It is always a matter of where you stand. Or where you are sitting. You can consider »Café Anzengruber« to be the best and smartest Viennese soccer *beisl* (pub). Especially when Austria and its new generation grab-bag teams play against Croatia – or, better yet, when the Germans once again get what , as everybody wishes ever since the legendary miracle of Córdoba in 1978: an elegant or totally authentic knockout. It doesn't matter from whom.

You can also see the »Anzengruber« as a watering hole replete with literati where you can watch famous authors imbibing. Newspaper columnists and the obligatory house poets have drinking contests without restraint and lay their wounded or nitpicking hearts just as uninhibitedly and loudly as their major successes on the bar counter.

Not only that, the »Anzengruber« is also the meeting place of night owl comedians who want to take a lukewarm shower in the residual audience and try out new gags just before bedtime… There are always fun things going on in this café. And it is an artists' pub; the galleries are just around the corner, full of tales and Bohemians constantly fluctuating between having a passion for life and being revolted by it. Almost all of the old »Wild Style« artists from Germany and Austria, the Viennese avant-garde in any case, have gotten drunk out of their minds here at one time or another, and have declared the »Anzengruber« to be their home base.

The café has been around since the late 1940s and has been owned since then by the same Croatian family, who have fast service in their blood. Everything runs like clockwork, and especially the heavy beer drinkers appreciate it when they hardly have a buzz and the next full glass has already landed on the table.

This turbo-paced boozing naturally only functions because the excellent food provides a wonderfully stable bedrock that can hardly be shaken.

Address 4th district, Schleifmühlgasse 19 | **Transport** bus 59a to Schleifmühlgasse | **Opening times** Mon−Sat 4pm−2pm | **Tip** Internationally known drinkers can occasionally also be found in the »Silver Bar« in the hotel »Das Triest«, Wiedner Hauptstrasse 12, (beyond the limits of the Viennese bohemia).

4__The Arena

All for one

Those who knew the old Arena remember it with wistful nostalgia. They were young then themselves, which is always a source of all kinds of warm nostalgia when looking back, and in the summer of 1976, when the foreign slaughterhouse in Erdberg was occupied by squatters, life seemed to still hold the possibility that someday, everything would be completely different and much better. The Arena was – at least for a short, anarchistic summer – the site of their own social utopia created back then out of the »Alternative Festival Weeks« – working together democratically at the grass-roots level with endless debates; although, when the debates were over, nobody could say exactly what they should actually do there in Erdberg.

Leonard Cohen, a folk icon of the late hippie era, declared his solidarity with the squatters and sang for them, as did the youthful Austrian singers Ambros and Danzer, and the Austro-pop-political band Misthaufen, during whose last, encouraging concert in the slaughterhouse the idea of never leaving made the rounds.

Nevertheless, the old hall was already torn down in October because ultimately, nobody was ready to throw themselves in front of the wrecking ball. Today's Arena has been housed in the neighboring domestic slaughterhouse since July, 1977, thanks to Social Democratic conflict-solving skills, and has evolved into Austria's largest alternative cultural center.

For some, the Arena is a museum of Viennese myths without which the whole subsequent alternative culture in Vienna could not have been possible. For others, it is an aging venue for events, run-down and only decoratively political, but still where the best non-mainstream acts perform. There are 450 events each year, and such diverse people as Katy Perry, Manic Street Preachers, Ringo Starr, Clueso, and the Arctic Monkeys perform in the large and small halls – open air, and, as a last resort, in a *beisl* (pub).

Address 3rd district, Baumgasse 80 | Transport U 3, bus 80a to Schlachthausgasse; tram 18 to Baumgasse; bus N75 to Arena | Opening times Office (advanced ticket sales) Mon–Fri 11am–5pm; Admittance to the events usually from 4pm | Tip If you are more interested in literature, then you should attend the events in the Rabenhof Theater in the municipal building of the same name in Rabengasse 3.

5 _ The Art Cell in the WUK
Creative minimalism

It is most likely the smallest exhibition space in Vienna and Austria and maybe even the world that can actually be entered and performed in. The »Kunstzelle« was conceived, created, and, for a long time, solely financed and also solely curated by the artist and WUK activist Christine Baumann. It is an old, discarded telephone booth (or cell) like the ones that used to be on almost every street corner in Vienna back in the days of analog telephoning; a sturdy iron box with a fixed rear wall and glass from top to bottom on the other three sides. This opens up a wide range of surprisingly good possibilities to the invited artists. In recent years, it became, among other things, a fold-out multiple-function sculpture resembling a miniature adventure playground complete with a barbeque area (created by Gruppe Anonim); a rampantly growing grass sculpture (by Katrin Hornek); with mirrors all around so that as many alternative WUK inner courtyard and outer world visuals as possible would find room in the cell (by Jörg Lange); armed as a weapon (by Andreas Dworak), and disconcertingly performed in by the street theater group Carpa, who crammed themselves, short of breath and sweating profusely, into the cell's barely two cubic meters of air space. It became a wetcell (by Markus Hofer) and once again, for a change, a telephone booth in which visitors could chat with unknown persons over a user-to-user connection to Zurich (by Matthias Bildstein).

Most of the works, installations, and performances are specifically created for the Art Cell, or their creation was first prompted by it. This also binds them temporally to this venue. Usually they are dismantled after two months and placed in the garish family album of the innumerable WUK activities.

The Art Cell now has its own budget, which is not equal in size to its importance, more symbolic than efficacious, but it turns the Art Cell into a real Viennese institution.

ct, Währinger Strasse 59 | Transport U 6, tram 40, 41, 42, bus 40a
asse/Volksoper; lines 5, 33 to Spitalgasse | Opening times daily
Tip The Kunsthalle Exnergasse (also a part of the WUK – workshops
e) is curated very openly; with a little luck, anyone who can may exhibit.

6__ The Augarten
Picnic park

Summer days in the Augarten are sometimes so perfect that they linger in your mind for a long time and, like a melody, you can hum them to yourself in fall, when the days begin to shorten once more. Everything is just right. The boule players are wearing straw hats and drinking white wine like in an old Gauloises ad; the people in the hammocks are dangling a leg over the side as if they were at home on Robinson Island; chess players are playing the Nimzo-Indian defense; young fathers are cradling their children as tenderly as if they had given birth to them themselves, and the mothers on the picnic blanket look as fetching as the naked woman in Manet's famous painting, *The Luncheon on the Grass*. There's Veltliner and white burgundy wine chilled to perfection, and rolls and triangularly-cut sandwiches as only served in the »Schwarzes Kameel« (Bognergasse) and at »Trzesniewski« (Dorotheergasse). People are perfectly equipped with a picnic basket and champagne bucket, or improvising in true Viennese style with things from the closest Billa store.

The former French pleasure garden in the old Danube floodplains was the favorite park of Emperor Joseph II (1741–1790), who was one of the most romantic souls to come out of the Habsburg Dynasty. Every year he had nightingales set loose there. Since the 30th of April, 1775, the park has been open to commoners as well. The first Augarten concert on May 26, 1782, was conducted by Wolfgang Amadeus Mozart, and ever since, the Augarten events belong to Vienna's summer highlights. Recently, and limited to three years for the time being, the art collector and patroness Francesca von Habsburg has opened the exhibit center »TBA 21« (Thyssen-Bornemisza Art Contemporary) in Gustinus Ambrosi's old studio; entrance on Scherzergasse. The conspicuous incongruities in the Augarten are also in the true Viennese spirit: still towering above every sensation of pleasure up into the strikingly blue picnic sky are the anti-aircraft gun towers of what once was the »Fortress of Vienna«.

Address 2nd district | Transport tram 2, 5 to Am Tabor; bus 5A, tram 31 to Obere Augarten-strasse | Opening times The park gates open from Nov–Mar around 6:30am, from Apr–Oct around 6am; the park closes at dusk. | Tip »Kino unter Sternen«, Movies under the Stars, is the summer film festival held in the months of July and August in the Augartenspitz.

7 The Badeschiff

All aboard

Swimming pool ships always look like the world is a little mixed up because instead of swimming in the river, which seems the natural thing to do, people swim in a boat that is floating on the river. At least considered from a distance, that naturally doesn't make much sense. Swimming pool ships are a relict from the time when rivers were still controversially used as sewers and were as toxic as the bile of a boarding house matron. Only the dumbest and toughest would dare to put a foot into the water. Or you had to be completely waterproof.

The Swimming pool ship between Schwedenplatz and Urania is not only a floating swimming pool with a sundeck and the illusion of an ocean voyage, it has its own beach that is around 2,000 square meters in size, a beach bar, and, on top of that, a gourmet restaurant and a nightclub that is one of the most popular in the downtown area. You could spend all day and all night here and never have to set foot on land. The »Holy-Moly!« restaurant has a current rating of two chef hats, meaning it belongs to the finest in Viennese society. In addition, the restaurant has dietary qualities that are normally only to be found in luxury health spas such as in Eugénie-les-Bains in France, where Michel Guérard came up with minimalistic nouvelle cuisine in the early 70s. The servings in »Holy-Moly!« restaurant are still so dumbfoundingly minute that it would presumably be impossible to gain a single ounce, so that you also always have that wonderful feeling when eating that you are doing something for your health.

When the swimming pool ship and the beach are fully occupied on hot days, some 1,200 Viennese are enjoying the fantastic view of the façades of the houses in Leopoldstadt and the Danube Canal right in the middle of the city. During the annual Viennale, the swimming pool ship is the film festival's headquarters and media control center.

Address 1st district, on Donaukanallände between Schwedenplatz und Urania | Transport
Public transport tram 1 to Julius-Raab-Platz | Opening times Pool (in summer) daily
10am–10pm, restaurant Mon–Sat 5pm–1am (kitchen until 10pm), closed Sun, hols;
Laderaum Club Wed–Sat 10pm–4am (depending on the program) | Tip The activities and
events held by the 100-year-old cultural forum in the »Urania« at Aspernbrücke are always
interesting. The Urania has its own observatory and a narrow bar terrace.

8 The Balcony of the Church on Hof Square

Dissolved ties

Nothing commemorates it today – no plaque, no memorial stone – and the bright baroque façade looks as if it were completely untouched by historical events. On August 6, 1806, the emperor's herald stepped out on the balcony of the »Church of the Nine Choirs of Angels« and proclaimed the end of the Holy Roman Empire. It had existed for 1,000 years, and had played a decisive role in the power struggles in Europe. Its beginning dates back to Christmas Day in 800, when Charlemagne was crowned Roman emperor by Pope Leo III, and for the first time, something like a concept of Europe took shape. His empire was reorganized and expanded during the decades of the Ottonian emperors, between 936 and 1024. »Of the German Nation« was added to the official German name of the Holy Roman Empire at the beginning of the 15th century. For the remaining 500 years of its existence, with the one single three-year exception of Charles VII, a Wittelsbach, this European superpower was ruled by emperors of the Habsburg dynasty. Now, Emperor Francis II had his herald proclaim that in his view, »The ties that up until now have bound us to the body politic of the German Empire are hereby dissolved.« If he hadn't, Napoleon Bonaparte would have annexed Austria.

Politically, the Holy Roman Empire was meaningless when it was dissolved. The national borders were redrawn nine years later at the Congress of Vienna, when around 200 larger and smaller European states negotiated Napoleon's legacy and their newly-found national identities under the leadership of Metternich, the Austrian foreign minister. Only in the evenings, when the balcony is illuminated by the lights of the Column of Mary on the opposite side, does it have something noble and theatrical about it. Then it looks like a grand and glorious stage. Its most recent actor was Pope Benedict XVI in September, 2007.

Address 1st district, Am Hof | **Transport** bus 2A, 3a to Bognergasse; U1 to Stephansplatz; U3 to Herrengasse | **Opening times** daily from 7am–noon and 4pm–6pm | **Tip** When you come out of the church, go to the right into Drahtgasse, which will lead you directly to historical Judenplatz (Jewish Square).

9 The Ballgasse

The way Vienna used to be

Once upon a time, there was a different Vienna. Small, with winding alleyways, and unorthodox in its layout. When the Turks were standing at the gates of Vienna in 1683, they were already standing within the city's boundaries.

Back then, the city didn't follow it's the effective and ultimately profitable lines that it expanded and cultivated in the 19th century; the boundaries at the time were still completely arbitrary and human. The needs were simple, and the courses of the streets usually conformed to natural conditions and downward slopes that could wash away unwanted refuse with the sewage water in the gutters.

The streets were as crooked as life, slow, and with one lane, because significant oncoming traffic was unimaginable. This period of time, when the streets were still winding, has a fairytale quality, a quirky coziness as in the paintings of the German Edwardian painter Carl Spitzweg, or the lighthearted scenes of the watercolorist Rudolf von Alt.

With the beginning of industrialization in the early 19th century the cities changed, along with their vital lines of transport traffic. The shortest route between A and B was defined by the formula that brought the most efficiency. The streets were made ruthlessly straight. In Vienna, all the new boulevards led in a straight line to the major train stations.

Ballgasse in the inner city is one of the last streets whose course is still completely the same as in medieval times, even if the buildings you see on the street date mainly from the 18th century. A little fantasy will take you back to the time when making a wish still worked. The pleasure of taking a few steps into the (car-free) past is sadly very short, but there is some fine compensation. At its end, when you come out of Rauhensteingasse, you'll pass out through a gateway onto Franziskanerplatz, one of the most beautiful and romantic squares in Vienna.

Address 1st district, Ballgasse | Transport U 1, U 3 to Stephansplatz | Tip the »Kleines Café« (legendary local classic) belonging to the actor Hanno Pöschl and the noble wine bar restaurant »Artner« can both be found on Franziskanerplatz.

10__ The Bohemian Prater

Back to childhood

It looks a little like someone forgot to close it down. Somehow, the Bohemian Prater has gotten out of its time, peeling and yellow like photos in an old family album. Before it really does disappear because the merry-go-rounds are no longer profitable and only the really young and really old children take delight in their own naivety and the harmless pleasures, you ought to visit it once – or one last time. Retirees sit in the cozy beer gardens and play. People eat till they are stuffed and talk till they are merry. At any rate, it is cheaper than in the city, and nowhere near as loud and crowded. The waiters know you by name, and the ham hocks are just as good as in the »Schweizerhaus« down in the big Prater. That's why whole families happily make their way in the heat of summer to this shady, comfortable old place.

It has been here for more than 100 years, and was originally an amusement park for the brick yard workers from Bohemia. The »Brick Bohemians'« Prater grew and shrunk again and again, was almost abandoned, and then once again revived. Today, it is being held back by what makes it so unique: the so seldom found carnival atmosphere that is immediately so familiar even if it's the first time you've been up on the Laaer Berg and gone behind the garden plots; the atmosphere you know from old films and children's books. It is a place full of nostalgic encounters that has something of portable radios and popsicles, of lottery booths and air baths. They are trying to save the place's dusty attraction in the present with small games of chance that promise huge rewards.

If the Bohemian Prater were actually to be torn down someday, the question naturally arises as to what should be done with the antiquated merry-go-rounds and carrousels. The best thing would be to declare the whole place a national heritage: a museum presenting the commemoration of the fantastic weekends of our own childhood, when we could do everything we wanted to.

Address 10th district, Laaer Wald 30C | Transport bus 68a to Urselbrunnengasse |
Opening times Ma −Oct daily 10am−10pm | Tip If it gets too loud for you despite the
contemplative nostalgia, there is peace and quite to be found in the newly designed Laaer
Wald Park.

11 The Bonbons

For a few more candy treats

One of the nicest shops, seemingly filled to the roof with candies, chocolates, and bonbons, is the store on Neubaugasse that first opened in 1936. It is now Vienna's oldest candy shop, and has that good smelling, secret flair that nestles so pleasantly in everyone's memory.

Candy shops are a part of Vienna like the coffeehouses and *beisls* (pubs). Unfortunately, they are in the throes of disappearing. There are fewer and fewer of them, even though they played a significant role in the socialization of Vienna. Here is where you get reward and comfort when you step into the subdued semi-darkness of the shop, shielded from the sun, and admire – at least as a child – the saleslady, who seems to own it all and pours with unbelievable precision the exact amount of ounces desired from the candy scoop into the little paper bag. Here is also an early opportunity to put one's charm and *schmäh*, the famous Viennese humor, to the test to get more than your finances allow.

The fact that you'll meet more grown-ups than children today in »Bonbons« is naturally due to the nostalgic candies on sale. Rum lozenges, bonbons filled with liquer, unshelled almonds, Florentines, and Deutschmeister chocolate are dusted with a wistful whiff of the past. Candy shops have always been the true places of our yearnings that are almost always intertwined with beautiful memories; seldom with toothaches and problems swallowing.

One's own childhood is omnipresent here, and that is why there are the timeless children's classics that everyone loves to stuff in their mouths, and the chocolate boxes tied with a ribbon and those elderly gentlemen's boxes of chocolates can be found in all sizes to suit all occasions.

Every holiday season is announced with the corresponding displays and decorations. It is then that »Bonbons« looks like a glittering treasure chamber, especially in the wintertime.

Address 7th district, Neubaugasse 18 | **Transport** U3, bus 13A, 14a to Neubaugasse |
Opening times Mon–Fri 9am–6pm, Sat 9am–5pm | **Tip** »Destille« is a special store for
adults offering fine whiskeys, rums and grappas, Neubaugasse 51.

12 __ The Botanical Garden

Plants are educational!

Normally, you come out smarter than you went in. That is primarily thanks to the little signs that identify each plant and inform the visitor of the name, family, genus, species, and habitat. You can observe the growth of about 11,000 species over an area of close to 80,000 square meters all year long.

You can become informed about their climatic and geographic requirements, and study how they are able to adapt – at times amazingly – to the very specific conditions in Vienna. Just like humans, some of the exhibits need an unheard of amount of manure or encouragement to thrive at all.

The Botanical Garden was founded under Empress Maria Theresia in 1754 as a »Hortus medicus« in which medicinal plants were cultivated and medical students were taught about their effects. Two trees that were planted under Director Nikolaus von Jacquin between 1768 and 1796, a plane and a ginkgo, are still growing in the park today, and have outlived not only the monarchy but two heavy bombardments in the Second World War, when a total of 40 bombs hit the garden.

The garden stretches between Jacquingasse and the park grounds of Belvedere. The several thousand daily visitors in this tourist epicenter in the baroque park between the two magnificent summer palaces of Prince Eugene of Savoy are amazed by the all-encompassing vista from afar of Vienna, with its increasingly quirky buildings.

As if by a miracle, the Botanical Garden is spared from this delightedly excited mass of people.

On average, only around 500 botanists, newspaper readers, preschool teachers, and plant enthusiasts (the numbers have already been storm-corrected since the garden remains closed on stormy days), disappear from view behind the man-high vegetation and in the wonderful avenue of 600 trees.

Address 3rd district, main entrance Mechelgasse/Praetoriusgasse | Transport tram O, 71, bus 77A, rapid transit S 1, S 2, S 3, S 7, S 15 to Rennweg | Opening times Main entrance from Jan 6, 9am −3:30pm, Feb 10am−4:30pm, Mar 10am−5pm, Apr−Sep 10am−6pm, Oct 10am−5pm, Nov 10am−4pm, until Dec 24, 10am−3:30pm | Tip Vienna's oldest tree, the »Thousand year-old Yew«, is at Rennweg 12.

13__The Bräunerhof

Waiting for Bernhard

The »Bräunerhof's« most famous guest is glued way up on the window. In the photo taken by Sepp Dreissinger in 1988, Thomas Bernhard looks totally likeable, nice, and comfortable, as if it were his time off, his hands in his pockets. He liked »Bräunerhof« so much that he made no secret of his aversion for it; and the coffeehouse's managers and waiters found Bernhard's literary aversions so charming that they printed the text from his book »Wittgenstein's Nephew« right on the menu.

»I have always detested the typical Viennese coffeehouse, famous the world over, because I find everything in it is against me. Yet for decades I felt at home at the Bräunerhof that was always against me, like the Hawelka.« The most famous café owner in Vienna, Leopold Hawelka, who, like Bernhard, has been immortalized on postcards, put it in a nutshell, »Bernhard is not a joy for nobody«. And, as was his nature, Bernhard was pleased.

For in the end, that's how he saw himself. Of course, there are a lot of Bernhard fans who snoop around in the »Bräunerhof« for the spot where the old grouch used to sit, and if you ask the waiters to show you the place of worship, they'll sometimes point over here and other times over there, depending on whether or not they like the person asking the question.

The waiters are, and Bernhard knew this as well, the nicest in the city. Though, admittedly, they don't always show it, and when they forget their genuine Viennese charm, which seldom happens, an icy wind blows through this cult site of recent literature, and most of the house-tamed guests disappear behind their newspapers.

The *fiaker* drivers have also caught wind of this Viennese curiosity and, with a gallant gesture of the chin toward the »Bräunerhof« und its poster of Bernhard, they grumble toward the amazed and totally unaware passengers in the back, »Very nice coffeehouse. Very famous«.

Address 1st district, Stallburggasse 2 | Transport bus 2a to Habsburgergasse; lines U 1, U 3 to Stephansplatz | Opening times Mon–Fri 8am–9pm, Sat 8am–7pm, Sun, hols 10am–7pm | Tip Vienna's best music shop, Musikhaus Doblinger, founded in 1876, has its premises in nearby Dorotheergasse 10.

14___ The Breitenseer Movie Theater

The last heroes

It isn't the nicest looking movie theater in Vienna, but at least it's the oldest, maybe the oldest in the world. Nobody knows for sure, and ultimately you can make of it what you will. It was first opened in 1905, and has been operating under that familiar name since 1909.

A specialty of the Breitenseer movie theater is the so-called Sword-and-Sandal movies, a term which critics mean to be derogatory, that is used to keep an important genre at an intellectual distance. The theater itself uses the term to advertise, as if it doesn't trust the quality of the old films – although cinematic passion almost always begins with adventure films. Not only are the sets stunning, and the straightforward and wonderfully uncomplicated heroes are impressive, oiled and flawless. Unfortunately, nothing has remained of the original beauty of the Breitenseer movie theater, and the plush and theatrical old movie house is completely missing after several renovations. That limits the whole pleasure naturally, and nothing is left for the nostalgic movie-goers, who make up the bulk of the aging visitors, to do than to set out on the journey into the landscape of their childhood without, in a sense, the corresponding nostalgic setting.

The auditorium has now become as barren as you can imagine rooms in a municipal building – robust and durable, but bereft of poetry. The poetry has to be in your mind and in your memories in which you search for the feelings and atmosphere of when you saw *Ben Hur*, *Hercules* or *Quo Vadis* for the first time, and sailed the seven seas with the buccaneers. These old sources of beautiful illusions are increasingly lacking customers (just recently, another old movie theater, the »Gloriette«, was forced to close). But the movie-obsessed owner, Anna Nitsch-Fitz, continues to promise to start the shows on time as long as just a single paying customer shows up.

Address 14th district, Breitenseer Strasse 21 | **Transport** tram 10 to Laurentiusplatz |
Opening times Show times Mon–Fri 6:30pm and 8:30pm, Sat, Sun 4:30pm, 6:30pm,
8:30pm | **Tip** The fan site for long departed Ufa stars is the Bellaria-Kino on Museum-
strasse 3.

15 _ The Café Goldegg

The monarchy and everyday life

Naturally, not everything is still original, although it seems so on first impression. The café was remodeled in the 1980s, made a slightly better suited to the tastes of the time, and the concept of what an authentic old Viennese café should look like determined the decor.

Today, despite a modern bar and a massive kitchen cupboard, it again looks as authentic as if very little had changed since its opening a hundred years ago. In contrast to the centrally located coffeehouses in the 1st district, not much is going on here. Only a couple of regular customers silently reading their newspapers or practicing their billiards skills. Sometimes you might find yourself alone, which is a rare pleasure for coffeehouse visitors in need of peace and quiet – no one is there; for a few minutes you can hear the motions of the waiters, and the cook in the kitchen pounding a schnitzel.

All alone like this, you can enjoy the absence of life and unabashedly take a closer look at the cast-iron coal oven that used to heat the rooms (a regular museum piece as beautiful as the one in the supposedly heritage protected »Café Jelinek«, Otto-Bauer-Gasse).

Right behind it, through the last door to the right, you enter Café Goldegg's little magic chamber, the fabulous-looking smokers' room, probably the coziest place in all of Vienna. It seems a bit similar to an oriental salon, and its misty opulence recalls the times when smoking, above all Arabic tobaccos, was a socially desired and generally respected pleasure.

Since the »Goldegg« hardly gets any casual customers, most of the guests know each other and limit themselves to small gestures of recognition and greeting so as not to bother anyone in their contemplative coffeehouse hour. That is probably the reason that the »Goldegg« is the favorite café of ex-punk Peter Hein, a Viennese by choice and lead singer of the legendary and still innovative band Fehlfarben.

Address 4th district, Argentinierstrasse 49, corner of Goldeggasse | Transport bus 13a to Argentinierstrasse | Opening times Mon–Fri 8am–9pm, Sat 8am–8pm, Sun 9am–8pm | Tip The sidewalk garden of »RadioCafé« in the ORF Radiokulturhaus, Argentinierstrasse 30 A, is a favorite meeting place of journalists and radio listeners in the summer.

16__ The Café Kafka

Crazy about Franz

He almost died in Vienna. Six weeks before his death in 1924, Franz Kafka, one of the most important German authors of the 20th century, was transferred from the Vienna University clinic to the sanatorium of Dr. Hoffmann in Kierling, today Klosterneuburg. Kafka died there of pulmonary tuberculosis at the age of 41.

There is little in Vienna commemorating Kafka. In front of the Grabenhotel in Dorotheergasse 3, there hangs a marble plaque that says, »Franz Kafka and Max Brod stayed here several times«. Laconic, terse, and vapid. All the same, you do learn that Franz Kafka slept there somewhere. Naturally, there are many Kafkaesque places in Vienna. The hulking ministries, the passageways und some staircases, the wallpapered corridors in the Palais and in the Hofburg. The »Café Kafka« is not a Kafkaesque place. On the contrary, it is comfy, nice, a little alternative, intimate, familiar, and one of the last biotopes of refuge for heavy smokers who inhale more deeply than Kafka ever could, even without cigarettes. Particularly because of the difficulty in breathing, at least in the winter (the windows are wide open in the summer), the café is a wonderful place to reflect about Kafka and his friend Max Brod, who was a successful writer at the time but is known today first and foremost as Kafka's literary executor and rescuer of his manuscripts. While still alive, Kafka, who had no way of knowing of his later importance, had stipulated the destruction of all his writings after his demise.

You should read Kafka's letters to his fiancées here in this café: the ones to Felice Bauer, Julie Wohryzek, and Dora Diamant. Kafka fell in and out of love, got engaged and disengaged repeatedly. In Kafka's Café, which wasn't always named after him – it was first opened in 1880 – there is a women between the movie posters on the wall smiling just like Kafka, whom Kafka probably would have fallen in love with when she was no longer Sissi: Romy Schneider, whose life was glamorous, yet similarly unhappy as that of Franz Kafka.

Address 6th district, Capistrangasse 8 | Transport bus 2a to Mariahilfer Strasse / Stift-gasse | Opening times Mon–Sat 8am–midnight, Sun, hols 10am–11pm | Tip »Jelinek« (not named after Elfriede, however), 6th district, Otto-Bauer-Gasse 5, is a nice supplement to »Kafka«.

17__The Car from Sarajevo
A global problem

The bullet hole on the righthand side is easy to recognize, even to-day. Around the hole, the paint is chipped away. This says little in the shooter's favor, but a lot about the penetrating power of the 9mm Browning pistol. This first shot fired by the 19-year old Serbian na-tionalist Gavrilo Princip penetrated the sheet metal body of the Gräf & Stift Phaeton and killed Sophie Chotek, Duchess of Hohenberg, the wife of the Austrian heir presumptive Franz Ferdinand.

The second shot hit the archduke and ripped apart his jugular vein. He bled to death. The archduke's uniform is also on display in a black, recessed display case in the so-called Sarajevo Room of the Heeresgeschichtlichen Museum (Museum of Military History). It is a strange circumstance of history that the chauffeur of the six-seater cabriolet, Leopold Lojka, was the only one not informed about a change in route. He turned to the right at the Latin Bridge in Sara-jevo as originally planned, was corrected, and forced to stop and put the car in reverse, thus halting for a moment in front of Gavrilo Prin-cip, who was waiting at the side of the road.

At first, Emperor Franz Joseph was not particularly upset about the death of his nephew. He is said to have commented, »One prob-lem less«, and when Franz von Harrach, the owner of the car, report-ed back to Vienna, the aging monarch, who, according to his own accounts, had been spared nothing in his life, asked, »And? How did the archduke deport himself?«

One month after the assassination, on July 23, 1914, Austria is-sued a 48-hour ultimatum to Serbia that the Serbs couldn't comply with, even if they had wanted to. British Foreign Secretary Earl Ed-ward Grey remarked that he had »never before seen one state address to another independent state a document of so formidable a charac-ter«. The war, which was later to become known as the First World War, began on July 28 with the Austro-Hungarian declaration of war on Serbia.

Address Heeresgeschichtliches Museum, 3rd district, Arsenal | Transport bus 69a to Arsenal | Opening times daily from 9am–5pm | Tip They don't only document the dark moments; most of the rooms are full of the glorious events of the Austrian military, such as the victories over the Turks, the Prussians, and the French.

18__ The Cemetery of the Nameless

Death can be lonely

A lonely cross in the riparian forest in the southern part of Vienna, in the Alberner Hafen behind grain silos and warehouses, marks the spot of the first of the old cemeteries where people were buried whose fate it was to die nameless – people without identities, people who took their lives or whose lives were taken and were cheated: the homeless, the unloved, the desperate, the dishonored, the lonely. A maelstrom in the Danube that no longer exists had washed them ashore.

In the second half of the 19th century alone, it is said to have been around 500 women, children, and men. Apparently no one missed them or made an effort to search for them.

The fishermen who lived at the time on the banks of the Danube buried them in a makeshift cemetery, with little ceremony but with the realization that at some point the bodies had to be put in the ground – if necessary without the rites the church would deny to possible suicides.

After the first cemetery was destroyed by flooding and ice floes, the one that exists today was built behind a dike. The last burial took place in 1940.

»Nameless« is written on most of the iron crosses, and standing in front of the graves, questions involuntarily arise about those lying here but about their existence, in most cases, not a clue remains. And while you perhaps pluck self-consciously at the weeds growing on the graves, you feel the primeval fear inside of having to suffer such a fate, from which no one is really safe. Whoever is forgotten and no longer has a name also has no history that counts and can be told. Not only have you disappeared into a wet and much too cold grave, but also your life story into a total void that cannot even be revived by the fantasy of later visitors.

NAMENLOS

Address 11th district, Albern 54 (guesthouse) | Transport bus 76a to Alberner Hafen | Tip The Alberner Hafen with its bizarre container sights is one of the favorite places of the artist, cartoonist, travel journalist, and occasional Viennese Tex Rubinowitz (*Rumgurken: Reisen ohne Plan, aber mit Ziel*).

19__ The Chelsea
Rock 'n' roll hearts

After a quarter of a century and more than 2,000 concerts, the »Chelsea« is something like the music club of the Viennese indie community. It was named after the London borough of the same name whose urban pop culture defined the music of the 1960s and 70s. Famous people who lived there included Mick Jagger, Bob Marley, and the Sex Pistols. The »Chelsea« was founded in 1986 on Piaristengasse as a post-punk and new wave orientated cellar club with strong roots in rock'n'roll; but in 1995, after being sued for eviction and noise disturbance, the club moved to the railway arches that were still grungy at the time, and picked up on pretty much every musical trend that has enriched the lives of the younger and older generations since then. The legendary – and occasionally strongly nostalgic – Indie disco nights are considered to be a specifically »Chelsea« creation which, upon closer socio-philosophic consideration, although an oxymoron, is precisely the reason that the level of fun is kept so fantastically high. Music nerds and dedicated music aficionados naturally consider these frolicsome evenings repulsive, and gray-haired vinyl fans have already dismissed the »Chelsea« as an »Indie Ballermann« (named after the Assi Disco on Mallorca). But in reality, this music club is beyond any musical reproach, because in its long 25 years, there came the real cream, at least in its early period, live at their start, like Soundgarden, the Toten Hosen, or even the British late bloomer I am Kloot. The »Chelsea« produced a lot of locally well-known DJs, music critics, and producers.

And since Chelsea founder Othmar Bajlicz, is also a midfield player and won the soccer championship with the team Wacker Innsbruck in 1974, the ball rolls on TV at every appropriate and sometimes irritatingly inappropriate opportunity – not only are the major games of the Champions League shown in an intoxicated, fan club atmosphere, but randomly picked bizarre encounters in the Second German National Soccer League are also watched.

Address 8th district, Lerchenfelder Gürtel, U-Bahnbögen (railway arches) 29–32 | Transport U 6, tram 2, 5, 33 to Josefstädter Strasse; tram 46 to Thaliastrasse | Opening times daily 6pm–4am | Tip the »rhiz«, U-Bahnbogen 37, is a nice little evening musical supplement to the »Chelsea«.

20__ The Church of the Teutonic Order

Still cool

The idea of the best battle and tournament-tested knights meeting to accepted courageous new members into their circle would be enough to excite any child. Whoever is old enough to have seen *Richard the Lionheart* or *The Black Knight* has an idea of how it would look: fanfares everywhere, colorful shields, cheeky squires, fierce competition, beautiful damsels, and grandiloquent words. As an adult, one is rather bemused that the Order of the Knights of the Golden Fleece, which was, after all, founded in 1430 by Philip III, Duke of Burgundy, in Bruges, still exists. Once a year, on the 30th of November, the holy day of St. Andrew, the last knights of the once most exquisite order of the Western World meet together in the Church of the Teutonic Order. In the beginning, the order had, along with good old Philip, only 24 handpicked members (in the course of the centuries, it became over 1,300). After the dukes of Burgundy died out, the noble association became the house order of the Habsburgs. The last Habsburg on the Spanish throne, Charles II, »el Hechiza-do«, »The Hexed«, died without children. His death ignited the War of the Spanish Succession, and the order was divided into two lines, a Spanish one of the Bourbons, and an Austrian one.

The order is named after the Golden Fleece of the ram of antiquity, Chrysomeles, who could speak and fly and was recorded in Greek mythology as the savior of endangered royal children. In deep gratitude, he was sacrificed, and his fleece was kept in a grove sacred to the god Ares. Not long afterwards, the superheroes of antiquity, Jason and the Argonauts, set off to find and steal the fleece. They vanquished the sleepless dragon that guarded it. One of the last to be admitted into the order was Nicolas Paul Stéphane Sarközy de Nagy-Bocsa, who is also known as the husband of the French singer Carla Bruni.

Address 1st district, Singerstrasse 7 | Transport U 1, U 3, bus 1A, 2A, 3a to Stephansplatz | Opening times daily 7am–6pm | Tip It is also worth seeing the order's treasure vault in the same building, stairway I, 2nd floor, open Tuesdays, Thursdays, and Saturdays from 10am to noon; Wednesdays and Fridays, 3pm to 5pm.

21___ The Collection Camp
A dark place

Everything is quiet. On a summer's day, Kleine Sperlgasse seems much like many other side streets in Leopoldstadt, with a lot of sunlight on one side and an equal amount of shade on the other, looking like a small town street a long way from the real Vienna. The fact that the 2nd district has been spiffed up and freshly painted for a couple of years now can also be seen here. Gleaming façades in a color trying to be the imperial yellow stand next to tired post-war plaster that had made the city so ugly up until 20 years ago that one could have believed that Vienna had been wearing sackcloth and ashes to atone for her sins.

The memorial stones set in the pavement in front of the federal high school in house number 2c are disconcerting, and you only notice them when you have practically stepped on them. An unusually open confession is on them. »In memory of all the Jewish children and youths that were excluded and ridiculed by their teachers, beaten, and spit upon by their fellow students.« Two pairs of brothers and sisters are named to represent all of those that were deported and murdered in 1941. Once upon a time, in a completely different Vienna, the famous dancehall »Zum Sperl« stood on this spot, in which Johann Strauss (the father) conducted an orchestra.

A few steps further is another memorial stone with »Sammellager« written on it and a small arrow pointing toward the courtyard of house number 2a. Back then, as today, there was an elementary school there. The school was closed in the spring of 1941, and the courtyard and its outer walls were secured with an electric fence. This camp, as was the one in Castellezgasse 35, was guarded by the SS. Their commander was the SS Unterscharführer (sergeant) Alois Brunner who was later condemned to death in absentia as one of the major war criminals. He was never caught. On October 9, 1942, Brunner reported to Berlin that Vienna was »Judenfrei«. Most of the Jews deported from Vienna went through these two collection camps.

Address 2nd district, Kleine Sperlgasse 2 A | **Transport** tram 2, bus 5a to Karmeliter-platz | **Tip** The »Way of Remembrance« through Leopoldstadt leads to more than 40 stations that commemorate Jewish life in the 2nd district and the victims of the Holocaust.

22__ The Crime Museum

And all its dead

An exact observer of Viennese sentimentality once called the Catholic festival of All Saints Day that is celebrated on the 1st of November the highest of all Vienna's holy days. The whole city gets on its feet and goes out to the cemeteries to remember the dead, who now make up the largest part of the population in Vienna.

This love the Viennese have for the dead naturally has its dark side as well. A surprising number of Viennese, both male and female, feel the need to knock off their marital partner, lover, neighbor, or janitor.

Considered in a conciliatory manner, this inclination could be termed as the impatient side of necrophilia. They eliminate the delays and clarify the situation with – pistols, knives, ropes, and iron bars; in earlier times, poison and acid were popular as well, in private but also in public.

There have been a conspicuously large number of shootings at train stations and in coffeehouses. Disappointed hearts vented their feelings in front of a gaping public, and others who had cultivated their hatred in long years of marriage dissected their victims into their anatomical components using saws and jigsaw cutters so they could transport them in the dead of night through the alleyways to the Danube or to the next garden plot.

The Crime Museum is a place that deals with these black depths of the Viennese soul. The privately-run museum displays, you could almost say »lovingly«, the instruments and the circumstances which in no case lead to the perfect crime.

But as a visitor, you will be confronted with the most familiar variations in word and picture of robbery and murder, rape and murder, murder by poisoning, patricide, and murders of prostitutes, sometimes with the original weapons. The dark chambers smell a bit damp and moldy, which enhances the mental proximity to the exhibits most frightfully.

Address 2nd district, Grosse Sperlgasse 24 | Transport bus 5a to Tandelmarktgasse |
Opening times Thu–Sun 10am–5pm | Tip What usually follows a murder is the funeral!
The Funeral Museum in the 4th district, Goldeggasse 19, shows and explains everything
about Vienna's lovely corpses and decoratively uniformed undertakers or *Pompfüneberern*,
as the Viennese used to call them, derived from the French *pompes funebres*.

𝕾𝖙𝖊𝖕𝖍𝖆𝖓 𝖂𝖆𝖓𝖞𝖊𝖐

23__The Crupi
Italian Neorealism

How can you get excited about a food store in which there is hardly anything to see and just little to buy? It is totally contrary to the universally known opulence of those Italian postcards with overflowing cornucopian delicatessen in which sausages, hams, cheeses and candied fruits seem to grow from the ceiling. Nino Crupi's place of business could just as well have been a peripheral scene in Pier Paolo Pasolini's *Accattone* or in Vittorio de Sica's *Bicycle Thieves*. It could also have found a place in Bertolucci's *1900*, a food shop defined by its limitations and its pathos of humility.

The oranges that lay poured out in the display window, like an »arte poverapoor art« spatial installation in a gallery in the nearby Schleifmühlgasse, are supposedly the best north of the Po Valley, and at any rate, the best that can be had for (little) money in Vienna. They come from Sicily – from the Simeto Valley at the foot of Mount Etna.

The memory of a marmalade made from them still pampers the senses unforgettably in the memory years later. The olive oil is also highly praised, as is the honey and the ham, which most of the shoppers call, almost without an accent, »prosciutto«.

In general, people like to place their orders authentically, sometimes in complete sentences, as if from a language guide – which probably has something to do with the aura of the shop, the shoppers in the Freihaus quarter, and with the rather quiet Nino Crupi, who belongs to the philosophical school of the stoics – or to the Epicureans.

He only sells what he knows, and also only when his friends produce it. Nothing else ever interested him, although there have been many offers from distributors and investors during the past nine years in which he has been running his business. In this respect, he has no idea what he will have in his shop tomorrow. Maybe a lot more, but maybe a lot less.

Address 4th district, Margaretenstrasse 3 | Transport bus 59a to Schleifmühlgasse |
Opening times Mon 2:30pm–7pm, Tue–Fri 10am–7pm, Sat 10am–5pm, closed Wed
in summer | Tip The coffee-roasting establishment »Alt Wien«, Schleifmühlgasse 23,
provides the fitting quality of coffee to complement Crupi's oranges.

24__ The Designlovers

Déjà-vu in retro-look

Who wants to paint according to numbers? Or live off-the-rack? Furniture that you have to assemble yourself is undoubtedly as practical as dried soup in a packet, and sometimes these quick assembly elements like the famous Billy bookcases from Ikea even have cult status.

All the same, they are not originals, cheap at best and practical to dispose of, because the first time you move, at the latest, you'll want to get rid of these glued-together chipboard gems.

Erik Ebner, a former weaver, made no secret of his passion for well-designed and correspondingly well-produced furniture; instead, he made a business.

For years, he collected old and beautiful furniture from estates and fleamarkets – pieces with a soul, furniture with history and stories, often battered and temporarily set aside, but always with a dependable core that you could build upon.

Ebner acquired furniture building techniques through autopsies and experimented with dyeing leather until he was able to reconstruct the originals, ecologically compatible and free of toxins. The problem cases were a particular challenge to Ebner's ambition, and so he created originals out of the worn-out, sagging ruins of chairs, some of them first rate.

That is why you will hardly find any unreworked original pieces (that have exorbitant prices due to the mania for vintage products) in his store, »Designlovers«, but rather very beautifully refurbished pieces for relatively little money.

Following the current trend, many Danish and Scandinavian designs are being offered; seating furniture by Arne Jacobsen, Alvar Aalto, and Verner Panton, and bookcases by Nisse Strinning. But you will also find club chairs based on Adolf Loos, Chesterfield sofas, cantilever and cocktail chairs, home accessories, and many lamps and chandeliers from the space era and the so-called rockabilly.

Address 6th district, Otto-Bauer-Gasse 13 | Transport U 3 to Zieglergasse | Opening times Mon–Fri 10am–6:30pm, Sat 10am–4pm | Tip The fitting sounds for the vintage furniture can be found in the vinyl shop »Rave Up Records« on Hofmühlgasse 1 (extension of Otto-Bauer-Gasse).

25 _ The Domenig House

With a full mouth

Is there such a thing as prophetic architecture? Nothing has yet been recorded in the history of architectural style, but it seems that the Graz architect Günther Domenig (1934–2012) established it in the 1970s in Vienna. Domenig architecturally anticipated what is today affecting the economy, culture, and, not least of all, the morals of the entire world: the bluff of the bankers and their impudent delight in disappearing, loudmouthed and callously, in glittering settings. Domenig constructed a bank building in Favoritenstrasse for the former Zentralsparkasse: conspicuously glittery, optimistically buoyant, with a certain urban aggressiveness like in a Mad Max film; postmodern plopped down between sober, unadorned post-war buildings that still date from a time when you had to count every penny.

An enthusiastic critic described the entrance that embraces the whole front of the building named after the architect today (the bank moved out long ago, and the building, including everything inside, is under heritage protection) as »a kind of snout structure«. The building actually does look as if it had choked on something, and so the construction can easily be seen as a metaphor for the huge appetite of the bankers and their own unique greed to feed it.

Domenig was naturally no moralist. As an architect, he is counted among the Deconstructionists, and so the »snout structure« can also be seen as something that the banks eventually will face and Domenig already suspected: the knockout by the swindled creditors.

This »biomorphic-allegoric apparition of bones, tendons, skin, scales, pipes, and arteries« (same critic) looks as if it had taken an allegoric uppercut, right on the chin.

Since the Zentralsparkasse moved out, the Domenig Gallery is now in the house, which is organized by the Favoriten Cultural Association.

Address 10th district, Favoritenstrasse 118 | **Transport** bus 14a to Keplerplatz | **Opening times** Mon, Wed, Fri 2pm–5pm | **Tip** One of the most impressive, major architectural feats in Favoritenstrasse is the Roman Catholic St. Anton's Church, Antonsplatz, which was inspired by St Mark's Basilica in Venice.

26__ The Donau City Church
The search for angels

Since its consecration in 1955, the Chapel of Notre Dame du Haut, a pilgrimage shrine by the Swiss-French architect Le Corbusier, has been an aesthetic benchmark by which subsequent modern church buildings are measured worldwide.

Not only the observers, those paying for the building, and the critics, but also the architects orientate themselves towards this unique design pointing the way far into heaven and the future by the otherwise controversial city planner Le Corbusier, who until then couldn't deny a certain tendency toward lifeless residential silos in his major secular constructions.

Heinz Tesar, the architect of the »Christ, Hope of the World« Church, also based his work on Le Corbusier. In a certain way, his church is a homage to his great role model, reinterpreted after half a century, among other things because his »Hope of the World« stands like a final possible refuge between high rises and isn't standing, unlike Corbusier's »Notre Dame«, on a hill. Tesar's church is more objective and more conceptional, a poetic functional space that nevertheless wants to comprehend the structure as Western meditation; as a place of peace and quiet but also of communication, which the cross challenges it to be. Tesar works with other materials and the visual experience that came after Le Corbusier. His church mantled with chrome steel is reduced inside and out to a few essential terms and metaphors that Tesar manifests in a daring, yet purist, style; an imaginative and equally complicated inclusion of light into the great wood-paneled interior of the church. In the evening and in darkness, it shines through circular windows to the outside.

A modern-day iconoclast wrote with a red marker on the images of the Way of the Cross that Tesar had sketched in black: »Out with this shit, this is absolutely nothing.« Tesar demanded that the commentary be left where it was.

Address 22nd district, Donau-City-Strasse 2 | **Transport** U 1, bus 20B, 90A, 91A, 92a to Kaisermühlen-VIC | **Opening times** daily 8am–8pm | **Tip** St. Mark's Church (»Russian Church«) in Wagramer Strasse was built by Russian prisoners of war in 1917 as a makeshift Catholic church. Evangelical and Coptic services are held today in house number 16 across from it.

27 _ The Edi-Finger-Strasse

Here comes Krankl …

… that is the way the unforgettable sports reporter Edi Finger led into the decisive seconds in 1978. Then he made the remark famous throughout all Austria that would become a familiar catch phrase, »I wer' narrisch.« (»I'm going nuts.«) Hans Krankl had scored a goal for Austria in the 88th minute for a 3:2. Then Finger smothered his fellow reporter, Rippel, with kisses, also his radio technician, »certified engineer Posch«, as he informed his radio listeners, and, a short time later, he would have also had loved to do it to the German »god of crossing the ball«, Rüdiger Abramczik, because he was standing all alone in front of the Austrian goalkeeper, ready to kick in the equalizer. »Atta boy, Abramczik, he flubbed the shot! Poor beggar, that won't make 'im too happy.« Even after over three decades, many Austrians still remember quite perfectly what they were doing on the 25th of July, 1978, at 6:30pm, the moment when Hans Krankl scored against Germany and sealed what the German boulevard press immediately called the »humiliation of Córdoba« and the Austrian press a »miracle.« After all, the Germans were the defending champions. Krankl had scored goals two and three for Austria, the first goal being generously provided by the German Berti Vogts. At the time, the two opposing teams didn't really care much, since both of them had already been eliminated from the competition and the host, Argentina, became the new world champion.

All of the details would have been long forgotten if it weren't for Edi Finger, who spontaneously made a monument of national significance out of Krankl's double. »After 47 years, an Austrian national team, and what a team, a world-class team, is in the lead against Germany.« The Germans were excited as well and voted Krankl's first goal as »goal of the month«.

Edi-Finger-Strasse in Floridsdorf is new and pretty, and located at its end, encircled like a crown by colorful, thoroughly upbeat houses, is Cordobaplatz.

Address 21st district, Edi-Finger-Strasse / Cordobaplatz | **Transport** bus 30a to Kummer-gasse | **Tip** The »Miracle of Córdoba« is always best celebrated with kindred spirits in one of the essentially tourist-free wine taverns (*Heurigen*) in Stammersdorf, which is also part of the 21st district.

28__ The Engländer

Charming fame

The »Engländer« has a lot going for it. For one thing, the fine wine and the occasionally excellent food (lunchtime is far above the usual level of simplification that is currently making its increasingly gloomy rounds in the Innere Stadt district).

Then there are the extremely capable waiters with their phenomenal memories for faces, names, and preferences. It is a known fact that most Viennese experience a delirious happiness that borders on the surreal when a waiter remembers exactly what their favorite drink is even after an actually inexcusable, at the least barely comprehensible, absence of half a year.

And, above all, what they don't like. As if they had just placed their last order yesterday.

And the patrons, naturally, speak for the »Engländer«. In general, they are normally of a finer cut of cloth than those in the other coffeehouses; only a nuance but a substantial nuance, settled, but always with a light air of Bohemian nonchalance that they wear like perfume.

And many of those present are also considerably more famous and important than others in other coffee houses. But no one makes a show of it. Including the waiters. Certainly not the famous and important. Of course, the fact is lost on no one that renowned artists and writers are sitting there: philosophers, film and stage directors, actors, and genuine party bigwigs. It is this mild urbane snobbery of taking things for granted that makes this café, which is actually a café-restaurant, so unique.

That is why you won't find a seat in the evenings. Sometimes not even at lunchtime. If at all, at the bar in front of the TV. Usually soccer is on because that's what the waiters want, and naturally the world famous writers and directors, who always like to keep tabs on this metaphor of life.

Address 1st district, Postgasse 2 | Transport bus 1a to Riemergasse; U3, bus 1A, tram 2 to Stubentor | Opening times Mon–Sat 8am–1am, Sun, hols 10am–1am | Tip Once a legend and today still one of the first class spots in the Innere Stadt district is the *beisl* (bar) restaurant »Oswald & Kalb« at Bäckerstrasse 14.

29__ The Erdberg bus Station
A cold wind

People not planning on taking a bus trip hardly ever come here. Beneath the elevated road of the Viennese south-east expressway, Austria's most intensely used autobahn, the view is relatively limited, and that view is gray: concrete, asphalt, and a dash of color on the many buses.

It is a practical place, but not pretty. There are hardly any traffic problems for the 50 bus lines that travel from here to almost every European country. They quickly get onto the roads leading out of Vienna. You can go nonstop from Erdberg to Berlin, Oslo, London, Paris, and Rome. But most of the travelers go east, back to their families and relatives in Sarajevo, Mostar, Warsaw, Kiev, Timisoara, or Split. On special occasions, there are said to be as many as 5,000 of them a day.

Despite that, the place isn't very hectic. At least there is coffee, frankfurters, and a few things for the long journey at the kiosk, and the saleslady seems to wordlessly understand all languages from outside of Vienna, or always correctly interpret hand gestures. There are no misunderstandings. The plastic tables in front of the kiosk match the gigantic suitcases and huge travel bags that are all checkered and rectangular and will be pushed into the buses' storage spaces. You wonder if the people here are following their tentative dreams, or are leaving them behind at this very moment. Their faces are seldom relaxed and, as so often, only the children look happy. Lines of destiny will intersect here, because this place is always the start and also the end of something.

The Erdberg bus station is thus by all means a very poetic place, but decidedly one for tough poems that sound like steel drums, a place for sandblasted prose that likes no varnishing. Road movies through old Europe and the even older Europe that lies eastward begin here. Endless journeys without borders, but then again, with some that are difficult to overcome.

Address 3rd district, Erdbergstrasse 200 A | Transport U3 to Erdberg | Opening times 6:30am–9pm | Tip The most famous traveler to Erdberg was King Richard the Lionheart of England. He was taken prisoner in 1192 by Leopold V, Duke of Austria, at the corner of Erdbergstrasse 41 and Schwalbengasse 17, and only released in 1194 after payment of a large ransom.

30__The Espresso Hobby

And in the evening, a plain black espresso

The Italian years are long past. When they began, deep in the 1950s, Europe's nerves of yearning were laid bare, and fantasies were dominated by Sophia Loren, Claudia Cardinale, and the Latin lovers, Papagalli and Gigolos – one big party in fantastic summer clothes beneath a sea-blue sky with lots of spaghetti and insanely romantic Capri fishermen. The »Italian style« seeped into the gray post-war world like fresh spring water, and whoever made it over the Alps to the south could hardly put their enthusiasm into words. Domenico Modugno did it in 1958 with his smash hit »Nel Blu, Dipinto di Blu«, that has remained a favorite to this day with its refrain, »Volare«.

Those who returned to Vienna from the sand castles of Rimini and the Mediterranean pizza grottos no longer had a craving for melange, einspänner (black coffee in a glass with lots of whipped cream), and *Kaiserschmarrn* (at least temporarily). Their new, unclouded attitude toward life manifested itself in Vespas, petticoats, and espressos. Drinking an espresso to the sound of jukeboxes while standing – a deep, dark espresso that also whipped the gelled hair into shape from the inside and sent the mind off in the direction of »vita nuova«.

One of the most beautiful memories of this time is the »Espresso Hobby«. It's a curious name, and today, after half a century, no one can explain conclusively how it actually came into being. In recent years, the tiny »Espresso« was remodeled almost back to its old original 50s outfit. That particularly appeals to fans of vintage and design. A replica of the legendary Faema E 61 espresso machine that is enthroned like a sculpture on the tiny counter and that is like the Venus de Milo of coffee machines, as beautiful as it is, dominates the room and sometimes the conversation as well. The coffee that flows out of it under high pressure as a thin black thread tastes almost as good as in the Neapolitan bars.

Address 9th district, Währingerstrasse 9 | Transport tram 37, 38, 40, 41, 42 to Schwarz-spanierstrasse | Opening times Mon–Fri 7am–10pm | Tip The »Weltcafé«, right around the corner at Schwarzspanierstrasse 15, uses only 100 percent fair world trade products; open daily from 9am to 2am, in July and August until 11pm.

31__Falco's Grave
Coming Home (Falco part II)

Measured by his importance, the monument is, of course, much too small. You might find it weird, wacky, super, totally off the mark, or a bullseye.

Photo-mechanically engraved in glass, he stands before his fans as big as life, with arms spread out and clothed like an angel; serious, heroic, fresh from the hairdressers and tiptop as always – like back then, somewhat pale and arrogant, just the way he liked to present himself as Falco, as a young Viennese. But his fans naturally know that in real life, as Johann Hölzel, he was a totally nice and funny guy. Almost one of their own kind. The names of his greatest hits that everybody knows here anyway are also engraved in glass: *Rock Me Amadeus* – Austria's actual national anthem – *Out Of The Dark, Junge Römer, Jeanny*.

His grave is one of the most lively pilgrim sites in the Zentralfriedhof: loaded with flowers, colorful, with petitions, small gifts, and major avowals spread about everywhere. People in silent MP3 devotion, since naturally the playing of one's own CDs and cassettes is not allowed; but, just as naturally, the fans would love to celebrate the ultimate Falco resurrection party here. It never goes beyond quietly singing and humming his songs, which gives them a slight trace of melancholy.

There is hardly anyone who doesn't have his picture taken with this great Austrian rock star and his steadfast forward gaze, or hugs or kisses him. The picture will be sent off immediately, looking as if Falco were actually and physically standing on his own grave, ready to take off at any moment.

He did actually die in one way or another in February 1998, shortly before his 41st birthday. He has been reproduced endlessly since then. So he can't die any more. Even if he were to, his fans would kiss him awake again.

Address 11th district, Vienna's Zentralfriedhof (central cemetery), Simmeringer Hauptstrasse 234, group 40, grave number 64 | **Transport** tram 6, 71 to gate 3 | **Opening times** Nov–Feb 8am–5pm, Mar 7am–6pm, Apr 7am–7pm, May–Aug 7am–8pm, Sep 7am–7pm, Oct 7am–6pm | **Tip** Resting behind Falco is one of Austria's most successful and influential musicians, Kurt Hauenstein (1949–2011), better known under his project name, »Supermax«, group 40, grave number 28.

32__The Fillgraderstiege
Ripe for films

These are, if you are to believe the verdict of 80 art scholars, Austria's most beautiful steps. In European ranking, they are right behind the Spanish Steps in Rome, the steps in Paris that lead to Sacré Coeur, and on Rhodes to the temple of Athena.

They were designed by a student of Wagner, Maximilian Hegele, whose best-known work is the remodeling of the central cemetery in 1910. In this architectural context, Hegele also built the Cemetery Church of St. Charles Borromeo that dominates the cemetery and that today is counted among the most significant Art Nouveau church buildings. The elegant morgue and the photogenic main entrance (»Gate 2«) are by him. Mayor Dr. Karl Lueger, who was known as »handsome Karl« and was influential in Vienna in many respects, was interred beneath the main altar.

Vienna's most well-known steps were opened in 1910, the Strudlhofstiege in the 9th district designed by Johann Theodor Jaeger. They are an imposing Art Nouveau structure that ranks higher than the Fillgraderstiege in the consciousnesses of most Viennese and tourists because Heimito von Doderer named his most famous novel after it. In contrast to the Fillgrader Steps, the Strudelhof Steps are sweeping and opulent, like the staging of an operetta, beautifully overgrown by vegetation and as romantic by night and snow as a stairway in a health resort.

The Fillgrader Steps' reduced visuals give them a somewhat stronger impression, pure and urban; completely of stone and iron, a very good setting for a city documentary film with an existentialist touch, and could eminate the appropriate feelings. Back in the 1980s, before the great relaunching of Vienna, the Fillgrader Steps were so rundown and neglected that they had to be partially closed off.

Today they are under heritage protection, just like the Viktor Matejka Stiege and the Rahlstiege in the 6th district.

Address 6th district, between Fillgradergasse 8 and 10 | Transport bus 57a to Laimgruben-
gasse | Tip The Raimundpassage (entrance Mariahilfer Strasse 45 and Windmühlgasse 18)
is a series of courtyards and passages that has a couple of interesting shops and ethnic cafés.

33__ The Film Museum

The myths of everyday life

Can there be love without love movies? Probably, but not in the sometimes bizarre forms and unrealistic consequences we know. Films totally determine our feelings, and an unscripted gesture is something you can't readily be sure of.

The universally popular act of giving the finger was made socially acceptable by Hollywood, as was kissing in front of a photo wallpaper, and whoever can become calmly lost in their own daydreams behind a shower curtain has never seen Hitchcock's *Psycho*. Not to mention *Halloween* and *Jaws*.

We ourselves have now become, in our actions, wishes, fears, and resentments, fit for the silver screen, and, in this respect, the film museum in the Albertina is the most important and most enlightening for people of today in Vienna's magnificent world of museums.

It is naturally much more than just an overgrown shoebox cinema. But most visitors are not aware of its cinematic technical library, Austria's largest; or of some 350,000 photos documenting the whole history of films; or its many film posters, movie scripts, press folders, and the ever increasing number of living and posthumous bequests of film directors and actors.

The average museum visitor just watches the films. The thematic series of films shown here are based on an archive containing close to 25,000 films. There is no better nor more well-founded selection anywhere, which has become an occasionally breathtaking monument to well-known and, now and then, also unknown actors, directors and producers.

Unfortunately, and unintentionally, the film museum is making the survival of the once large number of Viennese revival houses and repertory cinemas difficult. They are slowly dying because the last untaken cinematic niches they once occupied are being filled by outstandingly restored classic films.

Address 1st district, Augustinerstrasse 1 (in the Albertina building) | Transport bus 2a to Albertinaplatz | Opening times Office Mon–Thu 10am–6pm, Fri 10am–1pm; library Mon, Thu noon–6pm; box office, one hour before the start of first show | Tip The little Admiralkino in Burggasse 119, in the 7th district, has a very ambitious cinematic program.

film
museum

34_ The Flo Vintage
Clothes, people, stars

The term »Vintage« is part of the cultural technique of »mixing«. Not simply a term, it is more an association and a vague description of a condition that describes with the word vintage something original, and sometimes also only something original that is outdated, but above all, always something authentic. Vintage is decidedly different from »retro«, because retro is never authentic, but rather just covered – at best, a look; at worst, a fake.

Whoever considers themselves to be up-to-date on fashion cannot do without a certain amount of vintage. The trick is the successful balance of street wear and vintage, but even on official and semi-official occasions, the mix works simply because of its originality. For years, the American photographer Scott Schuman's insider's website, »The Sartorialist«, has been showing people worldwide, above all in the major fashion capitals, who don't wear clothes exclusively from the rack, but give their individuality a conspicuous wardrobe through unusual combinations of basics and antique clothing.

In the romantic 70s that followed the spaced-out, knocked-up 60s (whose accessories today are part of the basic vintage outfit), such ambitions were shaped by nostalgia, and so, when the original »Flo« opened in 1978, it was conceived as a boutique for nostalgic fashion. Now, after almost 40 years, »Flo's« stock comprises close to 5,000 articles of clothing dating from the period between 1880 and 1980, all flawlessly preserved and, in most cases, seldom worn.

In workmanship and esthetics, »Flo's« selection belongs to the best that the representative prêt-à-porter fashion of the 20th century had to offer. Also one-of-a-kind haute-couture articles are sold for relatively little money (compared to their original high prices).

International fashion designers now seek inspiration for their collections in »Flo Vintage's« comprehensive selection, and honest to goodness stars seek an exclusively individual look in »Flo«.

Address 4th district, Schleifmühlgasse 15a | **Transport** bus 59a to Schleifmühlgasse |
Opening times Mon–Fri 10am–6:30pm, Sat 10am–3:30pm | **Tip** If you like this sort of
clothing, visit »Vintage in Vienna«, Gumpendorfer Strasse, 10am–noon in the 6th district,
and »Vintage & Beauty«, Kirchengasse 26, in the 7th district.

35__ The Fluc

Above is below

It is probably wrong to only see things the way they are. It is more important to recognize the potential that is in them; in other words – to look at what could be made of them. The bosses of the old and new »Fluc« saw an ideal venue for Vienna's subculture and avant-garde in a pedestrian underpass that had become irrelevant and was to be filled in. Still today, in the accounts of many a visitor, the old »Fluc« that was directly opposite on the other side of the street and had to be closed for structural reasons was an absolutely incomparably heady place that had provided for the sharp-edged socialization of many young Viennese after 2002. It is part of the legend of the creation of the new »Fluc« that the visionaries themselves ventured into the grungy underworld with wheelbarrow and sledgehammer to create what they had envisioned.

In April 2006, the new aboveground »Fluc« was opened: a conspicuous, low-slung spatial structure in baby blue that was put together out of containers and wood paneling, but also structurally follows the concept of transformation. This targeted change of structures and forms can be seen as a kind of short program of »Fluc«. Change is everything! Half a year later, the subterranean Fluc-Wanne (the former pedestrian passageway between Praterstern and Würstelprater) was launched.

There hasn't been a day without an event since then; something is always going on 365 days a year. There are concerts, readings, performances, and art exhibitions, either above or below, and ideally both. Naturally not just the cream of the crop plays here, but ultimately, they are all worth talking about.

It never gets boring, at worst too hot, and that many a performer is more well meaning than well versed or even a virtuoso bothers no one really. The dynamic energy that is always present in the »Fluc« has been appealing to its musicians, performers, and visitors for ten years now.

Address 2nd district, Praterstern 5 | Transport U1, U2, tram O, 5, bus 80A, rapid transit S1, S2, S3, S7 to Praterstern/Wien Nord station | Opening times daily 6pm–4am | Tip »Fluc« and »Flex« (on Donaukanal, exit Augartenbrücke) fit together like love and marriage. Or a pot and its lid: good sound, great program, fast parties and, in the depths of the night, many aging adolescents who can't cope with getting older.

36__Fool's Tower

Dark souls

When you are suddenly standing in front of it, after passing through the last courtyard of the old general hospital, facing its now slightly decaying walls, facing this dark, fearsome, round building that the Viennese, with their sense for the odd, call »Guglhupf«, you want to have been anything but a crazy person in Vienna in the 18th and 19th centuries. And yet this practical round building was considered a modern affair. Emperor Leopold II (»here the first«, as can be read on the wall of the Fool's Tower) himself had personally had thoughts which he put into words about how lunatics in Vienna were to be put away, at least those that were officially certified: namely in 139 cells, in twos if possible, with a slanting floor for water and urine, and all of them in chains, with the exception of the sociable, the singers, and the flower lovers, but otherwise all the rest of them. And when the chains were abolished, it was said to have been at least 200 hundredweight of metal. Entering into the modern age was very difficult. Nevertheless, the »Guglhupf« was considered progressive, inspired by the spirit of the Enlightenment, because normally those that ticked a little differently were hidden in cellars and made invisible, worse than animals, because for society, they were not only troublesome and frightening, they were totally worthless to boot.

The passion of the Viennese to liquidate their own history was also aimed at the Fool's Tower several times. But it's still standing there, and since 1971, the exhibits of the Pathological Institute have been housed here. In the meantime, the collection is said to include more than 50,000 pieces, making the Fool's Tower the largest pathological museum in the world. The collections archive everything that is different and abnormal. People with two heads, for example, and cats with four back legs, extreme growth deformities, abnormal growths and gigantic tumors, eroded lungs, inconceivable kidney stones, but also heads with gunshot holes clean through them.

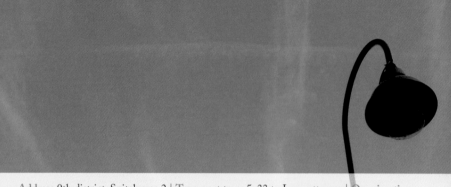

Address 9th district, Spitalgasse 2 | **Transport** tram 5, 33 to Lazarettgasse | **Opening times** Wed 3pm–6pm, Sat 10am–1pm | **Tip** The university campus in the courtyards of the old general hospital is a wonderful place to hang out, with garden cafés and a supermarket.

37__The Förstergasse 7

On the last day

There are no more bomb craters. The informer has probably long since disappeared from Leopoldstadt and has long been dead. There is nothing left to remind us of the tragedy – only a memorial plaque, as is often the case.

The plaque names the victims; the perpetrators have remained unknown to this day.

It is only known that they were SS men. On the 12th of April, 1945, a few hours before soldiers of the Red Army reached Förstergasse, they shot nine people in the bomb crater in front of house number 7 – people who had tried to survive in hiding and had almost made it in the face of all the adversity with which they had had to live as Jews since the so-called »Anschluss«, the political annexation into the German Reich in March 1938.

On the afternoon when they were denounced, and in the evening when they were shot, the Russian mortars could be heard here, and the news that the German troops were fleeing from Vienna over the last Danube bridge still intact raised the hope of survival to an unbearable height.

After seven years, they were not even half a day short of it. The Russians arrived around three-thirty the following night and searched the streets for scattered German soldiers. The bodies were still lying stiff amongst the rubble in the early light.

The memorial plaque is in memory of Nelly Blum, Arthur Holzer, Arthur Klein, Erna Klüger-Langer and her daughter Grete, Marie Margolin, Kurt Mezei, Emil Pfeiffer and Genia Schaier.

Kurt Mezei was only 21 years old. Before his death, he had been forcibly conscripted for a suicide mission, defusing the unexploded Allied bombs in the wreckage of Vienna.

His twin sister Inge had died in March during a bombing raid because, as a Jew, she was not allowed into a bomb shelter.

AM 12. APRIL 1945, WENIGE STUNDEN VOR DER BEFREIUNG
WIENS VON DER NAZI-ZWANGSHERRSCHAFT WURDEN

DR. BLUM NELLY, 54 JAHRE   KLÜGER-LANGER GRETE, 44 JAHRE
HOLZER ARTHUR, 59 JAHRE   MARGOLIN MARIE, 44 JAHRE
KLEIN ARTHUR, 56 JAHRE   MEZEI KURT, 21 JAHRE
KLÜGER-LANGER ERNA, 82 JAHRE   PFEIFFER EMIL, 66 JAHRE
SCHAIER GENIA, 48 JAHRE

VOR DIESEM HAUSE VON ENTMENSCHTEN SS-BARBAREN
ERMORDET.

NIEMALS VERGESSEN!

ISRAELITISCHE KULTUSGEMEINDE WIEN.

Address 2nd district, Förstergasse 7 | **Transport** tram 31 to Obere Donaustrasse | **Tip**
The writer (*Radetzky March*, *The Emperor's Tomb*), Joseph Roth, who was driven in despair
to the point of delirium over himself, the fallen Habsburg dual monarchy, and the Nazis,
had his first apartment in Vienna in 1913 around the corner in Rembrandtstrasse 35/5.

38   The Freudenau Racetrack

With neither emperor nor horses

It all began so nice and proper. The Vienna Jockey Club was established in December 1866 on English and French models; a very exclusive club that only accepted members who belonged to the recognized social elite.

Significantly, the club rooms were located near the Hofburg, in Philipphof on Albertinaplatz, which was destroyed in 1945. The Jockey Club's grand prize, the first Austrian derby, was already held in 1868 on the racetrack in Freudenau. The stallion Wissehrad, named after the old castle in Prague, won the derby. His owner, who today has vanished in the mists of society, had a swashbuckling-sounding name, Chevalier de Rama.

The following owners of the early derby winners are, however, indicative of the enduring exclusiveness of the Jockey Club and the racing events in Freudenau: Count Henckel, Count Széchény, Prince Louis Rohan, Count Esterházy, Count Ugarte, Baron von Oppenheim, Baron Rothschild, Aristide Baltazzi (he owned the Epsom Derby and Grand Prize winner Kisber and was the uncle of Mary von Vetsera who shot herself, together with her lover crown prince Rudolf, in Mayerling castle in 1889, precipitating the end of the Habsburg Dual Monarchy). A box, which still exists, was made for the emperor, and sitting in it, he watched the 1877 derby that was won by the Hungarian »magical mare« Kincsem (54 wins for 54 starts, a record unequalled to this day).

Freudenau is restored and freshly painted, but even if it does look like it did in the 1880s, it is still falling apart aimlessly, because no one knows exactly what to do with it. The last derby was run in 2003, the last race in 2008. Sometimes film scenes are shot here. The setting is authentic, and everything appears today as if the next derby is about to be held that was one of the social highlights of old Vienna back in the fine days of the emperor and into the days of the First Republic.

Address 2nd district, Freudenau 65, Rennbahnstrasse | Transport bus 77a to Gärtner-strasse | Opening times Since there are no races at present, there are no regular opening hours. | Tip The ever popular historic Lusthaus at the end of Prater Hauptallee is near to the racetrack.

39__ The Galleries on Schleifmühlgasse

In the labyrinth of art

A true lover and collector of art can't really be interested in material things; customarily, he already owns some. More or less without money, you are in the art world, as well, only an observer and an extra in a long waiting line; often creative and broke yourself, by all means with a friendly interest and great enthusiasm – when you are still young. With advancing age, you might possibly be entitled to a bonus card and one of the few seats in a museum. Passion does cost money, but one does not speak of money as long as one has it. Naturally, one likes to talk more about daring investments than about quick profits. Galleries are wonderful money machines. For one thing, you can throw away your money there, which particularly young, maladroit heirs are wont to do when they meet up with the right vacuum cleaner salesman. On the other hand, a lot of money can be made talking about artistic taste and art theory if you can smell it behind the aura of artistic intangibles. Everyone wants to get away from money; that's why they spend it. There are some 150 galleries in Vienna offering art and services just for this purpose. If you are interested in smelling the paint and the investment value when it is at its freshest, you can do it with entertaining analyses, evaluations, and small talk from any of the trendy gallery owners on Schleifmühlgasse.

Since the 1990s, Georg Kargl, Christine König, and Gabriele Senn have been enjoying the beautiful reputation of always being one golden step ahead of their time and the next trend. First exhibit discoveries for Austria, among them international blue chips, were made in their galleries, like the Chinese superstar Ai Weiwei, and the portrayer of British pop stars, Elizabeth Peyton. Cosima von Bonin, the German avant-gardist and the sculpture conceptionalist praised to artistic high heaven by critics, also had her highly acknowledged debut on Schleifmühlgasse in Vienna.

Address 4th district, Schleifmühlgasse | Transport bus 59a to Schleifmühlgasse |
Opening times Tue−Fri 11am−7pm, Sat 11am−4pm, the times for vernissages vary |
Tip The galleries in Eschenbachgasse and Seilerstätte also know what's up.

40__The Gallery of Literary Magazines

Nothing but words

Nowhere are there more, and nowhere are there prettier ones. Supposedly there are more than 130, nicely arranged in rows and archived. Naturally, not all of them are really significant, but literary magazines are of a complicated, sometimes irritatingly twisted and esoteric nature in which more hope and despair can be found than at the destruction of the world. Unfortunately, they are disappearing more and more out of the consciousness of even sympathetic, interested feature page readers, and if they weren't being constantly kept alive by artificial respiration, they would have probably suffocated. Before they are resigned to a last digital preserve by iPods and Kindles, you can take them in your hand in this wonderful selfless gallery, smell them, touch them, and feel them; leaf through them, and naturally also read and admire the effort most editors and layouters are still making today, knowledgably or in despite of not being knowledgeable.

The gallery is part of the »Alte Schmiede« literary institution. Whether one finds it meaningless or meaningful, attractive, out of place, or pretentious – the authors actually read here in an originally preserved old blacksmith's shop, in front of tools and forged objects, in front of an anvil and forge, as if they were artisans and part of the smithy trade. Despite this fully antiquated atmosphere that could be part of an open-air museum, the readings in the cellar vaults are considered to be exceptionally modern and up-to-date and among lovers of literature, occasionally ranking above those in the Literaturhaus (see tip).

The fact that sitting in the audience are all sorts of poets who personally knew and still know the veterans of the Viennese avant-garde is due to some extent to the closed system of such readings – whereby every new addition to the readers and listeners is not courted, but acknowledged in friendship.

Address 1st district, Schönlaterngasse 7 | Transport bus 1a to Riemergasse; U3, tram 2 to Stubentor | Opening times Office Mon–Fri 9am–5pm | Tip The Literaturhaus, Seidengasse 13, in the 7th district is absolutely worth a visit: exhibits on literary themes, a comprehensive library on Austrian literature since 1900 (c. 70,000 volumes), readings.

41__The Gänsehäufel

Among the Danube island sand and sun people

In the words of Helmut Qualtinger's omniscient basement denizen *Herr Karl*, a figure that scurrilously exposed much about the Viennese character, »Mir brauchn'S nix zum erzöhn, wei' i kenn dös ...(Ya don' hav'ta tell me, cuz I know all 'bout it ...)«, you don't have to tell any Viennese anything about Gänsehäufel because they know all about it. At some time, they have all been there, as children in any event, and later as well, even though there are more tranquil places to bathe, idyllic places and also those with nice views in front of you and below you. But no place is as crowded, loud, or as truly Viennese. The people are uninhibited and act as if they were at home in Vienna's largest public swimming beach. Among other things, because they have always gone there, or at least often enough to act as if they did. They are part of shade-seeking Vienna, almost naked and glistening, friendly to children, newspaper readers, sometimes slightly irritated, charmingly didactic, always mirthful, also outraged, sweaty and sluggish, by all means athletic, water crazy to an extent – simply put, just the way people are.

The 300,000 square meters is room enough for almost 30,000 Viennese. There are around 4,000 trees, 1,200 meters of beach, 500 beach huts and just under 300 beach cabanas that are something like Gänsehäufel pavilions, rented and defended by season ticket holders who spend the whole summer here and have more or less set up housekeeping. It all started more than 100 years ago, when Vienna's famous drop-out and proto-hippie Florian Berndl founded a kind of colony on Gänsehäufel and, as a former male nurse at Vienna's general hospital, wanted to refute orthodox medicine. Berndl buried his »patients«, the so-called Berndl fools, in sand. Peter Altenberg (1859–1919), who, as a coffeehouse man of letters, seldom saw the sun but always admired it, went personally as an eyewitness to marvel at this life-reforming and always golden-tanned Danube island sand and sun man. For him, the Gänsehäufel beach was a »fairytale of life«.

Address 22nd district, Moissigasse 21 | Transport bus 90A, 91A, 92a to Schüttauplatz |
Opening times May 2–15, Mon–Fri 9am–7pm, Sat, Sun 8am–7pm, May 16–Aug 31.
Mon–Fri 9am–8pm, Sat, Sun, 8am–8pm, Sep 1–18, Mon–Fri 9am–7pm, Sat,
Sun 8am–7pm | Tip Krapfenwaldlbad in Döbling, Krapfenwaldgasse 65–73, is almost
idyllic and has a beautiful view out over the hopelessly boiling city at the height of summer.

42___The Gartenbaukino

Light and shows

It is most beautiful when empty. 900 empty seats in the great 1960s design in front of a magnificent curtain, behind which is Vienna's largest movie screen. But this is a pleasure you can only have if you come very early and very quick. If you have time for cinematic devotions before the general popcorn excitement, you will sense that you are in one of the last and perhaps finest modern film cathedrals of the postwar period. It is most interesting when it is full: on the annual held Oscar Night, which is dominated by a large number of amateur actors, full of *schmäh*, enthusiasm, and disappointment. Or at the premiers of the Viennale and other film festivals, when the Gartenbaukino is the center of cultural night life, and real screen stars and directors get lost in the shuffle among the numerous functionaries.

On December 19, 1960, the Gartenbau opened with Stanley Kubrick's sandal epic *Spartacus*, and Kirk Douglas, the producer and pathetically shining leader of the slaves, came personally to the premiere to underscore the importance of the new theater. The Gartenbau was named after its legendary predecessor that was installed in 1919 in the exhibition hall of the society of the *kaiserliche und königliche Gartenbau-Gesellschaft.*

The new building was designed by the architect Robert Kotas, who is almost forgotten but so important in the history of Austrian movie theater design (he died in 1972). Of the more than 40 theaters he designed, only the Gartenbaukino remains, and is therefore worth a visit.

The former general public theater is now the most elegant of Vienna's repertory cinemas and, as in its beginnings, is accompanied by a constantly updated supporting program. The tradition of the short supporting films was revitalized, as well as the fashion shows so popular in the 1960s that always made a visit to the movies a socially relevant event.

Address 1st district, Parkring 12 | Transport U3, tram 2 to Stubentor; U4 to Stadt-park | Opening times Show times daily 5:45pm, 7:30pm, 9:30pm | Tip The municipal park located opposite is a source of incredible inspiration for screenwriters and filmmakers with its fabulous characters who spend their days here.

43_ The Gasometer City

Memories of the future

When, at the close of the 19th century, Vienna seemed to be growing beyond measure and, as was thought at the time, would even spread out past the Vienna Woods, the four circa 70 meters high gasometers in Simmering symbolized the direct entrance into this completely new and urban age. Hidden behind the crenallation-crowned masonry broken through on all floors by a variety of window shapes, were four gigantic gas containers, each with a capacity of close to 90,000 cubic meters. This made Vienna's gasometers the largest in Europe. They were constructed simply to ensure the nocturnal illumination of the megacity, which was to claim all of the energy for itself.

100 years later, four architectural firms remodeled the gas towers, which in the meantime had been placed under heritage protection, having long since been relieved of their gas-supplying function. A postmodern residential island was created, 220,000 square meters in size, with more than 600 apartments, an extra-long shopping center, its own subway station, and an entertainment center with multiplex cinemas and an event hall for 4,000 persons. In the beginning, the whole highly-polished ensemble was marketed as »G-Town« and the event section as the »Pleasuredome«, named after an old 1980's hit movie.

»Gasometer City« probably came 20 years too late. In the yuppie decade of the 1980s, it would have undoubtedly become the dream of the new market if the adaptation of old Industrial brownfields had become the status symbols of a futuristic viability, like sneakers, finger food, and coffee-to-go-cups. But instead of yuppie-dance pop, today the blues is played.

Many shops stand empty; in some corners it looks cheap and run-down, sorry consumers in corridors filled with curious sounds. The chic zeitgeist residents have to sweep up the *tristesse* left behind by a post-modern world that came to nothing.

th district, entrance Guglgasse 6 | Transport U3 to Gasometer City | Tip at Guglgasse 11, the »Hollywood Megaplex« offers current films in 15 theaters.

44_ The Gentzgasse 7

The leap outside

On March 12, 1938, soldiers of the German Wehrmacht, the SS, and the security forces marched across the Austrian border. Three days later, Adolf Hitler »reported« from the balcony of the Neue Burg to the frenzied Viennese on Heldenplatz square, »the admission of my motherland to the German Reich!«. On the following day, at about 10 in the evening, Egon Friedell walked out onto the balcony of his house in Gentzgasse and asked passersby to step aside, »I'm jumping«. It is benignly assumed he died while still in the air.

The bone-dry memorial plaque installed by the »Austrian Literary Society« assumes that Egon Friedell jumped »to his death out of fear of being arrested by the SA«. Could be. It is also possible that Friedell jumped out of an overwhelming loathing for SA men or out of horror in the face of a time that was ready to follow to its destruction some hysterical homeless nut who had lived for years in the men's asylum on Meldemannstrasse.

Friedell was born in 1878 as the oldest son of the Jewish merchant Arthur Friedmann; he failed to graduate from school, but passed the final school exam in Bad Hersfeld, Germany, studied in Berlin and Heidelberg, wrote his doctorial thesis on the early German Romantic poet Novalis, and became a cabaret artist. He was the artistic director of the »Cabaret Fledermaus« and in 1910 founded the scandalous »Intimes Theater« on Praterstrasse. Friedell, an entertaining and broadly educated writer, published his three-volume *A Cultural History of Modern Times* between 1927 and 1931 that is still published today. As an actor, he amused his audiences. The fact that Friedell was a Jew was unknown to his admirers, some of whom were Nazi sympathizers. »What's this I hear, Doctor? You're playing a Jew?« »My dear friend«, explained Friedell, »an actor has to be able to do everything.« His friend, Alfred Polgar, wrote that Friedell had lost his sense of humor for the first and only time in March, 1938.

IN DIESEM HAUS LEBTE
VON 1900 – 1938 DER ÖSTERREICHISCHE
SCHRIFTSTELLER u. KULTURHISTORIKER
EGON FRIEDELL
~ GEB. 21. 1. 1878 ~
HIER SPRANG ER AM 16. 3. 1938 AUS
FURCHT VOR DER ERGREIFUNG
DURCH DIE SA IN DEN TOD.

ÖSTERREICHISCHE GESELLSCHAFT FÜR LITERATUR

Address 18th district, Gentzgasse 7 | **Transport** U6, tram 40, 41, 42, bus 40a to Währinger Strasse / Volksoper | **Tip** At the end of Gentzgasse, number 127, the excellent »Restaurant Hill« (Jeunes Restaurateurs d'Europe) operates its own patisserie.

45__ The Geographic Center
The new middle

Vienna's beautiful new middle point can be precisely quantified: 48.220282, 16.3800575 degrees. People who know Vienna recognize immediately that only the southern tip of the Augarten can be meant, right next to the new hall that is built for the Vienna Boys' Choir.

For centuries, it used to be found in St. Stephen's Cathedral, the most beautiful and most eminent house of God there is. The cathedral was the mid-point of Vienna in every respect: socially, morally, philosophically, and in a way even militarily as a lookout; it was recognized as such by the attacking Turks in 1683 and wildly fired upon. The »Steffl« was the center of the old imperial and royal glory, and old Austria's lines of power and measurement ran directly into the cathedral.

Resistance was immediately raised against the new coordinates as soon as they were made known. For one thing, nothing happens in Vienna without a protest. That is due to the many experts who make their homes in Vienna. The method used by the »Middle Point Workgroup« in their calculations wasn't questioned in general – just their results.

The problem is that the southern tip of the Augarten dwells in the shadows and says next to nothing about Vienna. Instead of taking the simple mean values of expansion to the East, West, North, and South, they suggest relying on the middle point that would at the same time be the imaginary center of the area of Vienna if you were to cut out a map of the city, glue it on a piece of styrofoam, and balance it on a needle.

Then the new center would be located not far from the old one, in the former university, Bäckerstrasse 20, and could be fudged, with a bit of good will, to number 6, the home of the world famous schnitzel institute Figlmüller's restaurant. That would be fitting.

Address 2nd district, Augartenspitz | **Transport** U2, tram 2, bus 80a to Taborstrasse | **Opening times** The park gates are open from Nov–Mar around 6:30am, from Apr–Oct around 6am; closing times at dusk. | **Tip** The open-air summer movie festival »Kino wie noch nie« takes place in the months of July and August on the Augartenspitz. The films usually start around 9:30pm.

46 __ The Glasfabrik

Other people's furniture

The promise is a little vague, but it makes you curious right away. Antiques from four centuries are sold here; specifically those produced between 1670 and 1970, for the most part furniture, most of it unrestored and in the same condition in which the last owners, or their cellars or attics, left it.

This opens up the wonderful possibility of discovering something special and perhaps even at a cheap price. However, the people operating the Glasfabrik are dyed in the wool experts who recognize when there's a plum in their pudding.

Whoever steps directly from the nice but uniform world of Ikea into the big hall of the Glasfabrik will at first experience something akin to a small culture shock. Household furnishings can be totally exciting, wild and stimulating, and in times of yore, furniture was a robust matter built for the ages, with notches, springs and in solid wood, which is why they can still be sold today. Everything on sale here has been tested for sitting and handmade, and, in some cases, in use for decades.

There is a surprising amount of chairs among which you can sit down, also aesthetic ones. Visually, some are trash, like the lathed lamps out of Herr Karl's house of horrors, with imitation pig leather printed with designs as the lampshade.

The mute testimonies to bad taste and a petty bourgeois way of living are both touching and nightmarish, but perhaps they will someday experience a revival as a whacky joke lamp in a bobo's room.

Other things are pleasing at first sight and could add the crowning designer's touch to any vintage interior landscape, especially if it is faintly reminiscent of design classics by Loos, Hoffmann, or Eames that otherwise can be bought for tons of money, restored and in its original condition, at Lichterloh (Gumpendorfer Strasse 15 – 17) or Rauminhalt (Schleifmühlgasse 13).

Address 16th district, Lorenz-Mandl-Gasse 25 | Transport tram 10, 46, bus 48a to Joachimsthalerplatz | Opening times Tue–Fri 2pm–7pm, Sat 10am–2pm | Tip If you want it real cheap, you'll find furniture that is not beautiful but by all means serviceable in the ARGE Wien furniture warehouse, Lorenz-Mandl- Gasse 31–35.

47__The Golden Che

Without a gun

Almost everybody knows Che Guevara. His famous, striking likeness, stylized in red and black – the colors signalizing communists and anarchists – with a far-in-the-future look and a beret, is the face of revolution per se, on T-shirts and posters, as buttons and as graffiti, worldwide, when it is a matter of signaling resistance and eventually putting it into practice.

One of the conspicuous pop icons of the 1960s, like Jim Morrison and Marilyn Monroe, Guevara is the last leftist hero who has survived the fall of communism.

The famous picture of Che was shot by the Cuban photographer Alberto Korda when Che was 32 years old. Che has hardly aged since then. When Ernesto Che Guevara was shot by the Bolivian military in 1967, he was seven years older. But he still looked really good, a determined ascetic, delicate and self-confident, with the perseverance of a messiah.

The Comandante of the successful Cuban revolution and friend of its leader Fidel Castro, had tried in vain to carry the flame of freedom throughout South America, and, with his last remaining 14 faithful in the Bolivian highlands, was betrayed by the peasants whom he sought to liberate there.

We know this particular Che. His living sudarium. There are small variations of him with a longer beard, with a cigar and laughing, and surrounded by soldiers or women. He looks completely different in Donaupark. The only monument dedicated to him in Western Europe is here. It is the creation of the sculptor Gerda Fassel. Originally, Che was gleaming like gold. But he naturally wasn't golden. He just looked that way, like a beautiful memory. A little pomaded and a little stout, as if he had gotten older. In the meantime, he has darkened. But »He will live on in this monument«, one of the speakers at the unveiling had prophesied, totally Viennese and amiable.

ERNESTO „CHE" GUEVARA
1928 - 1967
REVOLUTIONÄR

„SOLIDARITÄT IST DIE ZÄRTLICHKEIT
DER VÖLKER"

„LA SOLIDARIDAD ES LA TERNURA
DE LOS PUEBLOS"

Address 22nd district, Donaupark | Transport bus 20B to Donauturm | Opening times anytime | Tip Memorials to the Chilean president, Salvador Allende, and the liberator of South America, Simon Bolivar, have also been erected in the Comandante's immediate vicinity.

48_ The Grandstand Cemetery
Party on the brink

There are soccer stadiums that are like cathedrals, such as Old Trafford in Manchester, San Bernabéu in Madrid, Giuseppe Meazza in Milan, or the Anfield Road Stadium in Liverpool. There are these brightly-lit cathedrals, these sometimes futuristic-looking bowls, and then there are little chapels, cryptic sites of a kind of primal community, and it can be argued where the true teachings of soccer are preached and, above all, lived out. In the Dornbacher Stadium of the three-time Austrian champions, the Wiener Sport-Club (also written Sportklub), the answer to questions of this kind is clear: here! And the answer is given even more clearly about the symbol-laden Grandstand Cemetery: only here! The Grandstand Cemetery has its name because the Dornbach cemetery lies behind it and the club was so often standing with one foot in its grave. Also, many a swansong was sung to the opposing team, as well as to money-grabbing professional soccer (outside Dornbach) as such. This is because most of the friends of the Grandstand Cemetery define soccer socially, as a mirror image, more or less according to simplified rules. Real beauty, they say, is in simplicity, and it really doesn't matter who wins when your own club comes up empty handed. In contrast to some bullheaded, brown-dyed ultras, as fanatical fans are called, most of the fans of the major Viennese clubs are shaded rather more red, are social, almost altruistic, often educated – not always, but in general.

The fact that they celebrate their own team's losses as well has to do with the myth, »You'll never walk alone«. This is particularly true in the dark hours of the day of the game. Only loving the winners would be too simple a game. It is the intricate dialectic that soccer demands. A victory can by all means be a defeat and a defeat a victory. So there is always something to celebrate. And when nothing else works, the best Viennese fans celebrate themselves, like those of FC St. Pauli or Swansea City FC.

Address 17th district, Alszeile 19 | Transport tram 10, 43, 44, bus 44B to Güpferlingstrasse | Opening times depends on the home games | Tip Playing soccer yourself is naturally more fun, traditionally on the Jesuitenwiese in the Prater, where the first soccer match in Vienna was played.

49 __ The Gravediggers' Graves
Two-time widow

The sometimes proverbial enthusiasm the Viennese have for death undoubtedly has to do with their enthusiasm for life. The often quoted »schöne Leich' (a beautiful funeral/nice corpse)« is not only an expression of generally aesthetic, but also of a moral and philosophical sensitivity. The art of living is revealed ultimately in death. People who understand how to live will make, in the end, a right presentable figure in one of Vienna's many cemeteries.

There are graves of honor and honorary dedicated graves for the great men and women of Vienna, a friendly upgrading or downgrading that shows that there is always a goal yet to be reached. The fact hurts that the most famous Viennese, who was in reality from Salzburg, came out empty-handed in the Viennese hierarchy of graves – without one at all. He was buried somewhere here in the St. Marx cemetery, anonymously in a mass grave and perhaps wrapped only in a simple shroud. The Mozart column in Marx Cemetery indicates the approximate place where Wolfgang Amadeus Mozart is presumed to have been buried. But the only one who could have known for sure was Mozart's gravedigger Joseph Rothenmeyer, who took his knowledge to his grave. But he did save Mozart's skull when digging up the grave to make room for fresh graves and handed it over in time to his successor, Joseph Löffler. Mozart's skull, or at least the one Rothenmeyer thought was his skull after eight years in a mass grave, came by way of the anatomist Grunzenberger into the collection of the Museum of Natural History.

Löffler married Rothenmeyer's widow, and now both gravediggers lie buried together in one grave, grave 149, not far from Mozart's memorial column. The graves are not numbered on the gravestones, only on a chart at the entrance to the cemetery. The gravediggers' common grave can be found in the continuation of the main walk, to the left of the graves of Count and Countess Chorinsky, in a side path, after about 15 meters.

Address 3rd district, St. Marx Cemetery | Transport bus 74a to Hofmannsthalgasse | Opening times Nov–Mar 7am to dusk, Apr, Oct 7am–5pm, May, Sep 7am–6pm, Jun–Aug 7am–7pm | Tip In another, today equally unknown grave lies the blind pianist Maria Theresia Paradis (1759–1824), for whom Mozart also composed.

50__ The Gurkerl Leo

Sour and yet funny

One day, he, along with his pickles and his *schmäh*, will be shipped off to the Vienna Museum. Or they'll put him under heritage protection right where he stands, lock, stock, and barrel, with the wooden barrels and cans of vegetables, the pickled gherkins, and the latest crop of sauerkraut. As the last of a dying breed, Leo Strmiska will then be a memento of how the Naschmarkt used to be. Or at least how it could have been, before the great *beisl* offensive when the market was still a market and not a twisted, if brand new Bermuda Triangle shoved across the Wienzeilen, as deep in the 1980s, the promenade between Rotenturmstrasse and Schwedenplatz once had been *the* disastrous place to go in Vienna One could think that the stand owners today are only the stagehands shifting the scenery for the crafty, well-seasoned community of restaurant and *beisl* owners.

They may be only picture book memories, but back then, it was more colorful, more alive, and somehow more real, a market for housewives and service people, cooks and gourmets. The stands back then were mainly small, improvised, just as the times used to be – authentic and sometimes charmingly unprofessional; when someone who was good at about everything only sold two or three products and, unlike today, did not march up with the inventory of a supermarket, waving around olives and chunks of cheese on a stick.

The fact that the Naschmarkt is still a world famous attraction (for housewives, service people, cooks, gourmets, and tourists) has to do with people like Gurkerl Leo, even though he has suffered as a stand owner as long as he has known this market because it is always too cold, too hot, and much too early every day. There is practically never any money in the till, although it is said that Leo Strmiska, in particular, never has to count every cent. For generations, his family has stuck to this irresistible market life, out of conviction, passion, and calculation, in which there are splendiferous pickles and continually new and surprising insights into life.

Address 6th district, Naschmarkt, stand 246–248 | Transport U 4 to Kettenbrückengasse; bus 59a to Pressgasse | Trading times Mon–Fri 7am–6pm, Sat 7am–5pm | Tip Urbanek, stand 46, not only offers top quality wines, cheeses, hams, sausages and pies that can be eaten standing up as at a snack bar, but also the news and rumors the customers bring in from the cabinet of curiosities that is Vienna are first class and exquisite.

51__ The Hardware Store

No loose screws

Most of the time in life is dominated by helplessness. At least when you want to do repair work around the house. It is often these totally simple things that threaten to defeat us and drive us to despair. That is because good advice is usually hard to come by, or not even available. Although there is an obvious solution for practically everything. After all, you are not the first person who wanted to change a lock, isolate a cable, repair a window, catch a mouse, or unclog a drain. It is easy to forget the mechanical fundamentals in the digital world.

So whoever in a perfectly normal turn of events unexpectedly finds himself helpless on a household ladder should search out Ph. Menning's, that rare and probably unique hardware store with its gigantic assortment of goods.

You'll find not only screws, nails, screw anchors, hooks and eyelets, individually or in packs, but also pepper mills, roof gutters, stovepipes, hand blenders, broomsticks, energy-saving lamps, garden hoses, coal shovels, flower pots, and espresso pitchers.

And naturally there are tools for every occasion, from the simple awl to punch a simple hole to digitally controlled drills to drill through particularly thick boards. But this list just scratches the surface.

All in all, there are supposedly a few thousand useful things stacked up to the ceiling here that you can always purchase at a reasonable price.

Even more amazing than the product range covering almost all areas of life is the encyclopedic knowledge of the sales personnel. They know simply everything. At least you take their word for it because everything sounds tested and obvious, somehow logical and sensible, and suddenly very familiar. If you felt like the ultimate idiot when you entered the store, you'll know how life out there functions when you leave.

Address 15th district, Mariahilfer Strasse 170 | Transport tram 52, 58 to Kranzgasse |
Opening times Mon–Fri 8am–6pm, Sat 8am–1pm | Tip Dr. Kurt Ostbahn, who has
a cult-like following, dedicated an album to one of the most unconditionally full-service
restaurants in Vienna: »Ein Abend im Gasthaus Quell«, 15th district, Reindorfgasse 19.

52__ The Heaven

Scattered around everywhere

The Viennese didn't create heaven themselves, but they did name an old summer resort on Pfaffenberg after it. You have a wonderful view of Vienna some 300 meters above the city, and on nice days, the Heaven above Vienna is so crowded you wish that many of the other visitors would go to hell.

The Viennese Heaven is not only beautiful, it is high, airy, and close to the Bellevue Meadow where, back in his day, Sigmund Freud discovered the meaning of dreams, and has had many a nightmare to answer for ever since.

There is also an esoteric place in Heaven with a didactically recycled tree of life circle with sound, whose meaning is vaguely orientated towards the signs of the zodiac. That naturally attracts people who want to draw strength here directly from the earth and the cosmos, mumbling crude incantations, throwing around ashes or coffee grounds, hugging trees, and celebrating the Big Mama on Walpurgis nights and at the solstice. That is why it smells of ancient Celts and herbal cigarettes and faded bliss, but also of soy curds and burnt Waldviertler sausages.

Hedy Lamarr wanted to be pretty close to heaven, in her star-studded film life and naturally also in Vienna. Born here as Hedwig Kiesler in 1914, she emigrated in 1937 and made a career in Hollywood as an actress. In her time, she was considered the most beautiful woman in the world (married six times), and as it later turned out, she was probably also one of the most intelligent. She owned a number of technical patents and invented the so-called Frequency Hopping Spread Spectrum (FHSS) together with composer George Antheil that is still used today in mobile communications. After her death in January 2000, she had her ashes scattered around the Heaven over Vienna, and so today we have that wonderful feeling of being completely surrounded by beauty.

Address 19th district, Himmelstrasse, corner of Höhenstrasse | Transport bus 38A, 43a to Cobenzl | Tip In the direction of Grinzing you pass the Bellevue Meadow where Sigmund Freud first dreamt the psychoanalytical dream in 1895. A memorial stone commemorates this fateful night.

53___The High Market Würstlstand

Sausages to die for

The Viennese sausage usually gives cause to contemplate life, and, when at a *Würstlstand*, most certainly out loud and with a full mouth, and therefore not always intelligibly to all of the bystanders. But that doesn't matter because at one end of the sausage or the other, everybody will be in agreement. There is not one subject about the length of a sausage that the Viennese is not capable of tackling extemporaneously. That is why you can get at the Würstlstand, along with the mustard and horseradish, the answers to questions you'd never ask yourself.

Viennese nihilism shows itself in the insight expressed over and over and several times daily that something is »eh wuurscht«, that is: it doesn't matter anyway. This credo encompasses practically all areas of life; the itty bitty ones and the great big ones like collapses of states, forfeited international matches, and undeserving names on the Decoration of Honor list: In the end, somehow, it's all the same anyway, it's all »wuurscht«.

And so it is that most Viennese have their favorite *Würstlstand*, which pleasantly distinguishes itself from all other sausage stands by virtue of the sole fact that it is their favorite stand. The *Würstlstand* on Hoher Markt has a special reputation: couples, passersby, churchgoers, the sleep-deprived, night owls, the nameless, and even famous, and therefore usually infamous, cultural icons swear by this particular stand. Perhaps it is due to the nearby fountain, the Verlobungsbrunnen, which inspires making wishes in the night, or due to the traditional Viennese smell of the *fiaker* horses that like to relieve themselves at the traffic light before they round the corner. For a short time at the start of the 20th century there even were two *Würstlstands* on Hoher Markt. One of them had to go, and the week-long dispute over the best sausage escalated in May of 1904. One of the sausage men first chased the other across the square and then shot him in the head.

Leberkäse

Address 1st district, Hoher Markt | Transport bus 1A, 3a to Hoher Markt | Opening times daily 9am–4am | Tip If the sausage isn't really all that important, then try the elegant stand-up take-away »Porcus«, Wipplingerstrasse 25, where pork is important.

54__ The Hofmobiliendepot
Living like crazy

People never cease to be amazed. »There are marvelous pieces among the furniture«, the Viennese journalist and drama critic Alfred Polgar had noted in an article in 1920, and praised the bourgeois grace of some of the German Edwardian period furniture on display here, calling it »virtually carpentered music«. But even if the Hofmobiliendepot has been displaying the Habsburg legacy of furniture since the monarchy, and the Depot has been a modern museum of Viennese interior art since 1998, one occasionally still gets the impression even today that what Polgar described in the same article was one gigantic junk room. That is not only because of the picturesquely chaotic »burlesque stage of furniture« on which everything that wasn't being used back then was stacked any old way on top of each other. In other rooms can be found, among other things, dozens of spittoons, chamber pots, chandeliers and candelabras taken from the rooms of the heir apparents, archdukes, princes, and princesses.

But as a »Musée sentimentale«, the Depot also displays such eloquent showpieces as the scales of the svelte Empress Elisabeth (Sisi) and the heavily padded wheelchair of the obese and therefore immobile Empress Elisabeth Christine, the mother of Maria Theresia. The sight of the wheelchair alone makes the viewer feel a degree of thankfulness for the monarchy's having been deposed. The end of the Habsburgs at the other end of the world is seen in the transport coffin of Emperor Maximilian of Mexico, whom the revolutionary president Juárez shot in 1867. Vice Admiral von Tegetthoff brought the embalmed emperor back to Europe on the expeditionary ship Novara in this coffin.

The historically so significant drama of Mayerling also has its own exhibit. Crown Prince Rudolf had shot himself there on January 30, 1889, along with his mistress, Baroness Mary Vetsera. In dry but precise words, it can be read on a plaque, »Deathbed of the Crown Prince. Oak. Side parts restored«.

Address 7th district, Andreasgasse 7 | Transport U 3 to Zieglergasse, exit Andreasgasse;
bus 13a to Mariahilfer Strasse / Neubaugasse | Opening times Tue – Sun 10am – 6pm | Tip
How emperors really lived can be marveled at in the tourist-jammed Kaiserappartements
(Imperial apartments) and the Sisi Museum in the Hofburg. Daily tours at 10am, 11:30am,
and 3:30pm.

55 The Hohe Warte Stadium

Remembering Jausen's opponents

Perhaps it was a very good decision by the magistrate to limit the use of the natural arena since its renovation in 2006. The sports stadium that once was the largest and most modern in continental Europe held 80,000 spectators.

Now there is only room for 4,500, and grass growing over the standing room. Keep off the grass! Perhaps the decision is good because the memories of the great time of Austrian soccer don't hurt as much.

At some point, people will still only remember the likeable kickers of First Vienna FC and the many victories of Vikings Vienna, who won the Eurobowl in American football and are repeatedly Austrian champions. This is the home of both teams.

At the opening of the stadium in June 1921, the First Vienna FC won 2:1 against the SC Hakoah Wien, the legendary pre-war Jewish soccer club that four years later was to become the first Austrian champion in the newly founded professional league.

But what was virtually Hohe-Warte Stadium's real golden hour came on May 16, 1931, when a more or less unknown team in Döbling ran out and sent the unbeaten Scottish national team home with a 5:0.

Only a week later, the team shot down the Germans in Berlin with deadly aim, 6:0, and the German press found the concept that summarized their formidable opponent in a single word and that still to this day endows all Austrian fans with undying fantasies: *Wunderteam*.

The Hohe Warte was the home base of this unusual team. Courted by many foreign clubs, the team dissolved after 21 months and 62 goals.

It was only possible to bring back the old glory of those wonderful bygone days one time, when the Austrian national team took third place in the World Cup in 1954.

Address 19th district, Klabundgasse | Transport tram 37 to Perntergasse; tram D
to 12.-Februar-Platz | Opening times for the games of First Vienna FC 1894 Wien and
the Raiffeisen Vikings Vienna (American football) | Tip The current hopes for another
Wunderteam are pinned on the games of the Austrian National Team in the former
Praterstadion (2nd district), named today after Ernst Happel, everybody's favorite grouch,
defender, and trainer.

56__ The Horváth Balcony
In our days

»Quiet street in the 8th district.« That was Ödön von Horváth's starting stage direction for his profound play, *Tales from the Vienna Woods*. Horváth names a house in this street with a doll clinic called »Zum Zauberkönig«. »Above the doll clinic is a balcony with flowers that belongs to the private apartment of the Zauberkönig.« The balcony in Lange Gasse 29 has been identified as the one Horváth had in mind when he wrote the play that takes place »In Our Days«. It premiered in November 1931 at the Deutsches Theater in Berlin. The folk actor and later Burg actor, Hans Moser (1880–1964), played the Zauberkönig.

Thirty years later, shortly before his death, Moser grumbled and mumbled his way in a heavy Viennese accent through this ambiguously cozy role. The menacingly sentimental Helmuth Qualtinger (who gave a permanent shock to the Viennese in 1961 as »Der Herr Karl«) was an emotionally touching Zauberkönig in the Vienna Volkstheater at the end of the 1960s.

»A meaningfully obscure grotesque, whose shadow is cast over things Austrian and beyond to the so-called universally human«, wrote the Viennese theater critic Alfred Polgar at its performance in Berlin. »A folk play and the parody of it. With ice cold wit.« What is undoubtedly Viennese about the people in this play, wrote Polgar further, »is their unity on the basis of venomous distain, their close, loving bond cemented by mutual contempt«. The *Tales from the Vienna Woods* has become a literary legend that, of course, not every Viennese appreciates.

Horváth's works were included in the »list of damaging and undesirable writing« in 1938. Horváth died the same year in exile in Paris, struck by a falling branch.

Since 1988, his grave has been in the Heiligenstädter cemetery (at the end of the wall to the left of the entrance, grave number 4).

Address 8th district, Lange Gasse 29 | **Transport** bus 13a to Theater in der Josefstadt | **Tip** The editorial office of the libertarian newspaper, »He and She. The Weekly of Cultural Life and Erotics« were located in house number 5–7 in Lange Gasse. Its chief editor and publisher, the journalist and mystery writer Hugo Bettauer (born 1872), was shot down there on March 10, 1925, by a conservative adversary.

57__The Hotel Orient

a few hours of pleasure

The »Hotel Orient« is so discrete that even after staying there you can't say for sure whether you really were there or not. Of course, there are permanent guests who would immediately deny ever having been there. Other Viennese, both male and female, who are given to revealing secrets, at least like to hint, even if they don't want to go into detail, that they had been there at least once during their married life. Maybe even often, and quite possibly regularly – in their thoughts at any rate. For example when they are planning on getting a grip on a potential crisis in their personal relationship. Some couples come out of love, out of the pure joy of play acting and masquerading, because they like the interior decoration and enjoy the idea of being in another period. Namely: as one of the last, truly beautiful hourly hotels in Vienna, the »Orient« is populated by marital and, of course, non-marital fantasies, with the intensive infidelities of old married couples playing a less significant role than the wish to mix some sultry perfume into a stagnating marriage and once again experience the »torrents of spring«. Naturally, everything revolves around mankind's favorite pastime in this pompously and opulently furnished hotel, whose numerous mirrors, especially the tilted ones and those on the ceiling, provide ample opportunity for self-reflection. And even if that is the main object, the well-insulated »Orient« is probably the ideal venue, right in the middle of the city, to simply and totally tune out, at best even alone.

Purely statistically (whatever that means), your perfectly average coitus lasts between three and twelve minutes. Measured by that, the three hours that the suites are available are more than enough, if you don't want to book them around the clock. The suites are, in the broadest sense, thematically accented and equipped with all kinds of furnishing whose practical purposes are only revealed by one's preferences. You can't make reservations, so all you can do is hope that a room is available.

Address 1st district, Tiefer Graben 30 | Transport bus 1A, 3a to Renngasse | Opening
times 24/7 | Tip If you need a stylishly opulent prelude to the »Orient« or a fitting end to
the evening, try the »Eden Bar«, 1st district, Liliengasse 2, which has been in existence
since 1904.

58__ The Joe Zawinul Park

Flowers for Joe Vienna

No one is ever forgotten in Vienna. Everywhere there are memorials and references, particularly to the living, if they are prominent enough, and, naturally, all the more to the prominent dead. There are in Vienna, and it is probably a worldwide exclusive, graves of honor and honorary dedicated graves, with the latter probably being a preliminary stage to the former. And then there are parks. There is a whole series of smaller and smallest parks in Vienna that have been renamed in honor of important men and women or are being named for the first time altogether. They are not always known to a wider public; for example: the operetta librettist Alfred Grünwald got a park, the neurologist Andreas Rett as well, the resistance fighter Grete Jost, and Alma Mahler-Werfel, who was married to world-famous men – to Gustav Mahler (composer), Walter Gropius (architect), and Franz Werfel (writer).

The keyboard artist Joe Zawinul is not only world-famous, he was the best and most prominent jazz musician that Austria ever produced. Born into a wildly mixed family of musical talents and laborers in 1932, he was a young fellow »with perfect pitch« at the music conservatory, played with the piano virtuoso Friedrich Gulda, was co-founder of the jazz band Austrian All Stars, and, for a short time, Ella Fitzgerald's pianist. In November 1970, together with the saxophonist Wayne Shorter, he founded the legendary jazz-rock formation Weather Report, which was hugely successful, equally both artistically and commercially.

Zawinul lived and worked most of the time in New York, where he also met his wife Maxine in 1963 in his temple of jazz, »Birdland«. He has, together with her, who, like Zawinul, died in 2007, a grave of honor in the Zentralfriedhof (group 33 G, grave 39).

Joe Zawinul Park used to be called, before it was one, Klopsteinplatz, named after a general in the Napoleonic Wars who held a bridge near Ennsbruck against the French.

Address 3rd district, Klopsteinplatz | Transport bus 74A, 77a to Rabengasse | Tip »The Box«, one of Vienna's discos with a tough doorman, is now where Zawinul's jazz club »Birdland« used to be (Hilton Plaza, 3rd district, Landstrasser Hauptstrasse 2).

Josef „Joe" Zawinul
(1932 – 2007)
der begnadete Jazzer-
Pianist, Keyborder, Komponist, Arrangeur und Bandleader aus Wien-
Erdberg hat in der Weinlechnergasse seine Jugend verbracht und
von hier aus seine Weltkarriere gestartet.

59___The Kaffee Urania

Idyllic as a postcard

For 50 years, the current operator, Herr Hubert, has been punctual-
ly opening at 8pm and closing again in the morning at six. The process
is always the same and dependable, and while he is still discussing the
Viennese world with his guests and speculating about the healthy
nicotine air in his coffeehouse (which has prevented every illness until now, at least in him), he arises, as if driven by automatic clockwork, to do what he has done his whole life long: close the curtains
at two, and whoever still wants to come into the »Kaffee Urania« has
to ring the bell of the »Freizeitclub Olympia«. Naturally, he doesn't
let just anyone in; actually only »club members«, but Herr Hubert's
door is more or least easy to get through.

In recent years, it has really only been people who live around the
corner and couldn't sleep, or students who have made a late discovery of the coffeehouse – friendly people who sometimes even serve
themselves when Herr Hubert happens to be busy with something
else.

In the beginning, he ran the night café with his mother, later with
his wife, and now, after her death, alone.

Since then, he has been collecting old Prater postcards. Otherwise, the loneliness of the long days would be too much to take. He
probably has the largest and most beautiful collection in Vienna. Real
treasures, as he says; rare motifs, actually something for the Vienna
Museum, possibly one-of-a-kind cards.

Whoever is interested can share in his appraisals and nostalgia, in
the changes in the Prater, in the world events between the merry-
go-rounds, and take a look at times that will never come again.

His café is one of the most popular places for birthday celebrations that begin the night before. That is why, along with cakes, beer,
and cold buffets, there are always merrymaking people toasting each
other.

Address 3rd district, Radetzkystrasse 24 | Transport tram 1 to Radetzkyplatz | Opening times Mon−Sat 8pm−6am (a club after 2am) | Tip It is pleasant to sit outside of and inside the »Gasthaus Wild«, Radetzkyplatz 1.

60 _ The Karmelitermarkt

Only the affluent …

Nobody used to want to go here. The Leopoldstadt was dark, particularly in the postwar years, burned down and half destroyed, curiously abandoned in Vienna between the Danube Canal and Praterstern. All in all, a rather gloomy spot with a grand but also sad past. In recent years, the Second District has been experiencing a Bohemian-like revitalization, and with it the old center around Karmelitermarkt and the Untere Werd, where the first Jews settled a couple of hundred years ago. On the Sabbath, when the market is usually the busiest, the old history of this quarter also occasionally parades by in the form of the many Orthodox Jews from Eastern Europe, who again live here. They walk about in their own isolated world, clothed in heavy black silk or in the symbolic white of the burial shirt, filled with a remote dignity, solemnly, slowly, on their most beautiful day of the week, between home and prayer house.

During the week, the marketplace is rather quiet and a bit boring, with a couple of old residents from the neighborhood. But on Saturday, when the elite of the organic farmers sell their biologically correct products along with their multifaceted slow-food philosophy, and you can hardly stop reflecting about life, the market becomes what is probably the most expensive of all the markets in Vienna and is always the most dependable meeting place of old Leopoldstadt's new, creative middle class that has provided the district with a booming property market and a brand new façade.

The friendly back-up power generators are turned on for the weekend; no hectic, a lot of hugging and easy, smiling gestures, along with intensive greeting and breakfast rituals. Madonna-like mothers holding immaculately dressed children up to the high snack bar tables beside fanatically security conscious fathers, who sometimes still have their bicycle helmets on their heads or look like picture book gardeners with straw hats and gunny sacks.

Marchfelder
Solo Spargel

Klasse I

½ kg: 5,00 €
1 kg: 9,50 €

Address 2nd district, Karmelitermarkt | Transport bus 5a to Tandelmarktgasse | Opening times Mon–Fri 6am–7:30pm, Sat 6am–5pm | Tip The Georgian market restaurant »Madiani« belonging to the cookbook author Nana Ansari, demands Zen Buddha-like patience on occasion because of its seemingly endless waiting times, but it is worth it for the unusually exquisite food.

61__ The Key Symbol

Locked doors

On the 3rd of December, 1940, Baldur von Schirach, Gauleiter and Reich Governor of Vienna, received a communiqué from Berlin informing him of the decision to deport the Viennese Jews. »It is intended to resettle 10,000 Jews in the General Governorate (occupied area of Poland) by May 1941. The selection of persons for the resettlement in the General Governorate will be carried out family by family by the Central Bureau for Jewish Emigrants in Vienna. The persons selected for the transport in question are to lock their living quarters, after which they will be sealed by the Secret State Police. The apartment keys are to be handed in. Every apartment key is to be provided with a pasteboard tag. The apartment, the name of the apartment owner, and his date of birth are to be written in legible writing on the tag.«

The *Gedenksymbol Servitengasse 1938* by Julia Schulz unveiled in 2008, 70 years after the so-called Anschluss (union), makes direct reference to this order. 462 apartment keys are set in the ground under glass on the corner of Servitengasse and Grüntorgasse, each with the name of the Jewish resident in this street who was still living there in 1938. Insofar as they had the financial option, they emigrated.

On November 10, 1941, the borders of the German Reich, and that included Austria, were closed for refugees. In October 1942, the Central Bureau for Jewish Emigrants reported that Vienna was »judenfrei«.

The keys that can be seen in the sculpture were provided by the current residents.

They are a symbolic invitation to those that fled or were deported to move back into their old apartments again. But, as it is so often the case, the facts speak their own language. About 70 percent of the Jews deported from Vienna were murdered in the extermination camps or died during transport.

Address 9th district, Servitengasse | Transport tram D to Schlickgasse | Tip Lying buried under the high altar in the Servitenkirche on the other side of the street is Octavio Piccolomini (1599–1656). He was the commander of Walleinstein's personal guard, and played a decisive role in his murder. Walleinstein was the supreme commander of the imperial troops in the Thirty Years' War.

62__The Kirchweger Spot

A right blow

»The opera's ass« is what the Austrian writer Thomas Bernhard has Paul Wittgenstein say what he sees from the terrace of the »Hotel Sacher«. Paul Wittgenstein was the »most passionate opera lover Vienna has ever seen« and »had to be taken to the insane asylum at Steinhof at least twice a year«. It was precisely on that spot, on the 31st of May, 1965, that the retiree Ernst Kirchweger was beaten up by a rightwing extremist. Three days later, he died of his injuries. No plaque on the rear of the Opera commemorates the first political murder victim since the Second World War in otherwise so gladly commemorative Vienna. Kirchweger had taken part in a demonstration by students and former resistance fighters against anti-Semitic tendencies, and attended lectures at the University of Vienna.

Kirchweger's funeral, which preceded a rally on Heldenplatz, became the biggest antifascist demonstration in Austria. Kirchweger was a Social Democrat and had fought on the side of the Red Army after 1918. During the Nazi period, he worked for free labor unions in the underground, ended up in a concentration camp and sympathized, after the war with Marxist-Leninist cadres, which made him, at least after his death, a venerated shining light of the extra-parliamentary left. The municipal building Ernst-Kirchweger-Hof in Favoriten (Sonnwendgasse 24) was named after him, as was the house occupied in 1990 in the 10th district, Wielandgasse 2 – 4, which was formally owned by the Communist Party of Austria and that since then considers itself as the only really autonomous cultural center in Austria.

Thomas Bernhard wrote about this place and his friend Paul, who was a relative of one of the world's important philosophers, Ludwig Wittgenstein: »For hours we would sit on the terrace of the Sacher hotel and accused. We sat with bowls of coffee and accused the whole world and we accused it down to the ground.«

Address 1st district, Philharmonikerstrasse (opposite »Hotel Sacher«) | **Transport** bus 3a to Walfischgasse / Kärntner Strasse | **Tip** »Reinthaler«, Gluckgasse 5, behind Albertinaplatz, is one of the last grass-roots town *beisls* (pub), which most certainly would also have appealed to Ernst Kirchweger.

63__ The Längenfeld

How they learn to love the bombs

It is the garden of pleasures. A subway embankment with an historical significance to the city at the old Längenfeldgasse subway station that today has disappeared underground. It is a public transport industrial wasteland of particular charm and perfectly suited, under constant bombardment by so-called seed bombs, to grow anew to downrightly wild beauty. Seed bombs are implemented like the classic revolutionary Molotov cocktails: formed out of a mixture of seeds, loam, peat, topsoil, and water, they can be thrown, in handy sizes, everywhere in the city, even onto hard to reach places. Since, after all, the whole city is supposed to bloom, and the no man's land between tracks and industrial buildings, on bridges, embankments, and traffic islands are to be transformed into a kind of community garden where everybody can sow and harvest as the spirit and need moves them.

Längenfeld is the mother of all the guerilla gardens in Vienna; a subversive place under rainbow and pirate flags with a lot of folk and reggae music, where the fruits of alternative urban dreams are harvested. It is all about land acquisition and freedom, about spaces of self-determination, and about autonomy. The illegal city improvement advocates and vegetable producers meet on Längenfeld for their nightly commando operations, to check out target areas in the districts, or to cultivate this steadily expanding urban garden. It is still only being tolerated by the city magistrate, not protected. That is why the guerrilla gardeners also sometimes guard the field, which is also always an occasion for an old sit-in-style session.

Guerilla gardening came into being in the 1970s in New York and has since then become a worldwide phenomenon. Besides the politically motivated activists, there is an ever increasing number of middle-class guerilla gardeners such as those in Huberpark (16th district) who are concerned about the beautification of their immediate living space.

Address 12th district, Längenfeldgasse | Transport U 4, U 6 to Längenfeldgasse | Tip
Recently, the planting activities of the guerilla gardeners have spread to the Prater. If you
have an eye for it, you will discover tomatoes, bell peppers, and kitchen herbs wildly planted
in the most unusual places.

64__ The Last Judgment
Burning souls

It is hard to believe, but the world-famous altarpiece by Hieronymus Bosch, *The Last Judgment*, isn't a latter-day copy. It is probably actually the original and therefore a major work of the master, even if it was never finally determined whether this triptychon didn't follow another work that King Philip I of Habsburg had commissioned Bosch to do in 1504.

At the end of a great hall it stands, opened up like a divine promise, a cryptic picture full of apocalyptic chimera in purgatory, enthroned between some not insignificant but not really significant pictures, a heavyweight in art history that one would expect to be in an art history museum and not on the first floor of an art academy.

Originally, so it is assumed, it was part of the collection of Archduke Leopold Wilhelm, a possible heir to the throne, the field marshal in the Thirty Years' War, who saved Vienna from the Swedes, and a bishop with several prince-bishoprics, who collected Dutch and Italian masters as an art patron and whose estate today can be found in the great museums of Europe.

Eventually, Bosch's *Last Judgment* came into the possession of the now forgotten Count Lamberg-Sprinzenstein, who gave his own extensive collection of exemplary masterworks to the Academy and its students in 1822, never realizing that the value of Western art believed at the time to be set and irrefutable, would, only a few decades later, balloon beyond belief.

The students soon lost their interest in Lamberg's bequeathment, and today even more so. That important collection is the Academy's family silver (which is, although highly valued, for all intents and purposes unsellable) and is of no use to the current students.

They would, for understandable reasons, rather learn from the works of Johnny Meese, Martin Kippenberger, or Herbert Brandl.

GEMÄLDE
GALERIE

Di – So 10 – 18 Uhr
www.akademiegalerie.at

MEISTERWERKE
DER EUROPÄISCHEN
MALEREI

Address Gemäldegalerie der Akademie der Künste, 1st district, Schillerplatz 3, 1st floor |
Transport tram D, 1, 2, bus 2A, 57a to Burgring | Opening times Tue – Sun, hols
10am – 6pm | Tip The Academy's art library is a must-see.

65__ The Laundromat in Karl Marx Hof

Forwards, comrades!

Looking back, it isn't easy now after almost 100 years to imagine that radical optimism which fired the workers between the two world wars, despite a worldwide depression, when they assumed they could be able to develop a culture wholly their own. They developed their own ethic that sharply distanced them from the so-called Lumpen-proletariat below and from the bourgeoisie above. The man of the future would be the man in overalls. The workers prepared for the class struggle in solidarity tenant associations, cooperative societies, cultural associations, and sports clubs, a struggle they would win with the backing of the Soviet Union.

Back then they could never had foreseen the rapid effect of petty bourgeois expectations that soon would seep into the municipal buildings and transform the bold, closed fist of the class warrior into an open hand on the take.

One of the most splendid symbols of this brief heroic time is the Karl Marx Hof. Not only because it was built like a 1.2 kilometers long shield of houses through Heiligenstadt, but because it was defended for a long time by its residents during the Civil War in February 1934. The attacking Austrian Armed Forces were even forced to bombard the Hof with artillery in order to subdue it. The paramilitary leftist protection league couldn't strategically hold it militarily. Its leader, the worker Emil Svoboda, was captured and hanged a few days later.

The laundromat in the Karl Marx Hof is today a museum that commemorates with remarkable exhibits the history of the working class in Vienna and specifically in the Karl Marx Hof. The outline of a worker's apartment painted on the floor shows where the great idea of a workers' culture failed: its concept was much too small from the beginning.

Address Waschsalon No. 2, 19th district, Karl-Marx-Hof, Halteraugasse 7 | Transport Public transport tram D to Halteraugasse; lines U4, 10A, 11A, 38A, 39A, to Heiligenstadt | Opening times Thu 1pm–6pm, Sun noon–4pm | Tip Not far beyond Heiligenstadt, in Nussdorf, Beethovensteig leads through the vineyards to a couple of nicely located restaurants.

66_ The Lingerie Shop in the Archiepiscopal Palace

A lot underneath

The ways of the Catholic Church are inscrutable. In this way it resembles God, whom it seeks to emulate. And so one can only speculate why the church administration had contractually stipulated that the lingerie shop in the Archiepiscopal Palace, in the passage to Wollzeile, directly across from the cathedral museum, must always remain a lingerie shop, and may never be rented out to a third party. Perhaps it has to do here with the attractive visual proximity of sin, as it is well-known that sin and its absolution are the top concern of ministers and their guilt-ridden congregations. It all started with Adam's and Eve's fig leaf. Not just the sweaty toil after the somewhat exaggerated expulsion from paradise, but a series of nocturnal amusements began as well that were inspired, not least of all, by the fig leaf.

The lingerie by Lola Luna, for example, which can be purchased here: tiny innuendoes captured in high quality lace that can be seen as being directly in the lineage of the original leaf that still grew back then.

After all, the desire to refine and sublimate are vital motors of every civilization, and give them a breath of paradise. It equally requires the art of concealment and omission to raise the senses and desires to a climax. Sophistication is an inseparable part of the erotic, its essence and its goal – which is why a shameless society only knows shockingly naked and somewhat short-winded sex. The bishops are aware of this too, of course.

That is why fine undergarments have been sold since 1931 in this shop, which is as large and intimate as a walk-in closet: real nylons, French bodices, handcrafted sleeping masks (you can bet no one falls asleep with them on) and corsets.

Address 1st district, Stephansplatz 6 (passage to Wollzeile) | Transport U1, U3, bus 1a
to Stephansplatz | Opening times Mon, Tue, Wed, Fri 10am–7pm, Thu 10am–9pm,
Sat 10am–6pm | Tip The selection at »Tiberius«, 7th district, Lindengasse 2, recently
includes fashion, but originally was concentrated on fetish.

67___The Lion of Aspern

Sad losers

The great battles have naturally all long since been fought, and the poster patriotism of times past is today more historical and something for the display rooms of the military history museums. Public places are preferably kept unemotional, and Archduke Charles, riding on Heldenplatz toward the Hitler balcony, already appears to be the biggest display of triumph that is allowed a victor. And so it is that the Triumphal Lion of Aspern in front of St. Martin's parish church looks rather distraught, almost as if he were crying. Ultimately not a bad interpretation because, after all, some 50,000 soldiers died between Aspern and Essling in May 1809. A prosaic place with an »Archduke Charles« street intersection and municipal building, a larger-than-life benedictive Christ figure, and a direction sign to a pizza service. Also not missing is a little pooping cardboard dog admonishing not to leave doggy doo lying about.

Archduke Charles waited in the lowlands of Lobau for Napoleon's army, which until this point in time was undefeated. Napoleon wanted Vienna. And if his stepson, Eugène de Beauharnais, had been quicker in getting to the Danube with his forces, his direct invasion would have probably been a success. The battles around and in Aspern, mainly around the parish church of St. Martin, were so fierce that the small village changed owners nine times, and only the daring of General Johann von Hiller, who, in retrospect, was proven to be one of Austria's most brilliant strategists, finally brought the completely destroyed village of Aspern under the control of the Austrians. Napoleon was defeated for the first time and withdrew. The Archduke did not pursue with his army, which can be interpreted as a realistic estimation of his own strength or else as a missed opportunity. Some six weeks later, on the 5th and 6th of July, another battle was fought, this time at Wagram, which Napoleon was able to decide in his favor and subsequently dictated his conditions to the Austrians.

Address 22nd district, Heldenplatz 9 in Aspern | Transport bus 26A, 97a to Siegesplatz in Aspern | Tip There is a diorama with 8,546 figures recreating the battle of 1809 in the Schütt-kasten (granary) in Essling, 22nd district, Simonsgasse.

68_ The Lobau

Let's go swimming, ladies!

It is easy to imagine how Herr Karl – the often quoted character unforgettably created onstage by the rotund actor Helmut Qualtinger, with modern variations still roaming the streets of Vienna today in large numbers – with his voyeur hat on his yellow press newspaper in his hand, fat and decidedly filthy, leering at the ladies as they go into the water. The headline is from him; that is taken from his *schmäh* humor. He, of course, didn't swim. In the early 1960s, people were pretty much uptight, as was Herr Karl when he drove to the Lobau with buttoned-up shirt collar, more to gawk than to swim. Today, since it's practical, the naked people already arrive naked, only in socks and tennis shoes because of the pebbles, but with a coolingbag. Whoever marches through the Lobau should count on seeing people lying on the grass in the idyllic spots as if they had just plopped down there, stark naked, and sometimes quietly munching away. This is because of the long tradition of anarchy that is at home in the Lobau. Even back in the 19th century, Viennese outlaws did whatever they wanted there. The authorities would have only gotten their feet wet. At the start of the 20th century, it was more the sun worshippers and sex reformers who camped out on the meadows and in the underbrush, read Karl May, and lived from hunting and gathering. Whoever thought the workers' swimming pools were too expensive or too crowded and much too embarrassing as well, found his happiness outside in the many pools, ponds, and cut-off meanders in the Lobau.

Recently, these cut-off meaners are being reflooded to prevent the Lobau from drying up. The Lobau is part of the last major alluvial forest in Europe, and the City of Vienna has an almost 3,000 acre share of it – which probably makes Vienna the only major European city that can still claim the remnants of a primeval forest. The Lobau has been a national park since 1996. Close to 5,000 animals and 600 varieties of plants are protected here. And the naked people give everything an almost paradisiacal touch.

Address 22nd district, Nationalparkhaus, Dechantweg 8 | Transport Lobau and the Lobau Museum: bus 91a to Panozzalacke | Tip The National Park House explains and documents the development of the national parks.

69__ The Loos Bar

The mother of all bars

Naturally, no one in 1893 could ever have imagined the results of the trip. Unknown and more or less penniless, the 23-year old Adolf Loos set out to visit his uncle in the new world, as unknowing, apprehensive, and awkward as Karl Rossmann in Kafka's novel, *Amerika*.

When Loos returned to Vienna in 1896, he set out with the intention of freeing the self-satisfied Viennese with their opulent and still very imperial lifestyle from their visual junk rooms. Loos saw a dangerous explosive not only in their plum dumplings that continually threw them off their balance, which was precarious anyway. His essay »Ornament and Crime« was an attack that cut deep in the ornamentally lathed table leg of the time. Ornamentation was nothing more than an archaic original sin that architects, designers, and consumers dragged around with them, the conspicuous mark of Cain on the forehead of primitive contemporaries whose purest and most genuine embodiment was that of the worst tattoo-adorned felon, the lover of ornamentation per se, whose life's goal could be nothing other than perfidious murder.

Naturally, the Viennese looked at it differently. And so Loos, measured on his significance as a theorist of modernity, was able to leave relatively little trace in the cityscape. The »Loos-Bar« is one, and probably the finest.

The »mother of all Viennese bars« opened back in 1908 as an American bar and in fact had so much visual class that it went down through the decades totally unperturbed and unaltered, although it is actually much too small for a real American bar, namely only 27 square meters in size. In accordance with Loos' axiom, »reduced to the maximum«, the bar was reduced to its original size in 1995 after several turbulent nightclub years (with real bar girls). Since then, you'll find there, as cosmopolitan barflies will gladly confirm, the best cocktails in the city.

Address 1st district, Kärtner passage 10 | Transport U 1, U 3 to Stephansplatz | Opening
times Sun–Wed noon–4am, Thu–Sat noon–5am | Tip a permanent exhibit in Loos
Haus, the architect's major work, provides information about the construction and history
of the house, its uses, and its changing owners; 1st district, Michaelerplatz 3.

70__ The New Brazil

The guesthouse garden colony

Brazil has always been a European fantasy – which doesn't only have to do with the uncomplicated women, the sun, the samba, and all the short Adidas pants that they can wear there without embarrassment on any occasion. Brazil was also exotic a hundred years ago, like the paradise where wild thoughts make their home, and even wilder feelings of freedom and adventure. It was the country of settlers and colonists, of dropouts and those seeking social alternatives, and so the gardeners with allotment plots, who only made it to the outskirts of the city in the evenings and on weekends, liked to call their garden allotment colonies »Brazil«.

When Vienna's most famous dropout Florian Berndl was forced by the municipal authorities to leave the Gänsehäufel in the 1910s that he had more or less discovered and built up into a little settlement of anarchists, he founded opposite the island a new, even more temarious garden colony of fearless sun worshipers and borderline cases, which he named, in line with the preferences of the time, »New Brazil«. That, at least, is one version offered by the myth of its origin. Another says that a once determined bunch of industrious Viennese, who actually wanted to emigrate but through all kinds of misfortune and yearnings only made it to the old Danube and to swimming pool lifeguard Berndl, found it to be so beautiful and wildly romantic there in the alluvial land around the Danube that they simply forgot to travel any further.

New Brazil, or »Neu-Brasilien«, actually is one of the most beautiful places in Vienna. It is a good place to sit and eat, look at the Old Danube, and, naturally, at other people's plates who might have a better spot directly on the water. The preferred place to sit in the eponymous *Gasthaus*, which is actually the garden colony's old shelter house, is right next to the water because of the view and, naturally, also because of the old dreams of foreign lands and a carefree life that still find their way into our daily lives.

"NEU BRASILIEN"

Tel: 01/2031 292

Address 22nd district, on the lower Old Danube | **Transport** bus 93a to Steinbrecher-gasse | **Opening times** *Gasthaus* Mon–Sun 11am–11pm | **Tip** The workers' bathing beach in the Arbeiterstrandbad Strasse is still popular with emigrants and those that didn't emigrate.

71__The Number Five
The World's Fair line

It groans and moans, creeping and rumbling between Westbahnhof und Praterstern: the number five, Vienna's oldest line. Even today, the tram route essentially follows the former north transversal route that was partially opened for the 1873 World's Fair. In January 1897, it became the first electric line with its own power source, and thus a celebrity with the curious Viennese. Everybody wanted to take a ride and be part of the miracle of driving horseless and at a walking pace through the city with the thrill of having a couple of 100 volts over their heads. People rode on it more for entertainment than out of necessity, and sometimes again today (the viewless underground combination of U 3 to U 1 is naturally much faster). So the ride itself was and therefore usually is the destination. The other destination – the one at the end of the route, the Würstelprater – is also rewarding. Back then, it was still a totally fantastic world, full of sensational attractions and unimaginably blissful joy.

Even today, it takes the number five close to 40 minutes to complete its eight kilometers-long route. A lot of time in an increasingly hectic city, which is why the route is only ridden all the way to the end by enthusiasts. The ride is the best in the old red streetcars that have been in operation for 40 years and started to be replaced by modern trams in 2007, and it is also relatively sporty on the hard wooden seats. Evening drivers occasionally chase the old number five – when the streets are halfway clear – at top speed through the six districts in which it has stops.

The route runs behind the showcase parts of the city, and you get a continually entertaining and often illuminating view into semi-official Vienna without its makeup. It goes from Westbahnhof in Rudolfsheim-Fünfhaus through the mixed middle class districts of Neubau, Josefstadt, and Alsergrund over the Danube Canal into the languishing gray of Brigittenau to then come to an iron-scraping halt at Praterstern curve in Leopoldstadt.

Address travels between Westbahnhof (15th district) and Praterstern (2nd district) | Travel times daily from Westbahnhof in the direction of Praterstern beginning at 5:06am (weekends at 5:08am) until 12:33am; from Praterstern to Westbahnhof between 4:58am and 12:08am | Tip If the trip becomes too uncomfortable, you can transfer to the bus line 13a at the Laudongasse stop. On the wild stretch between Skodagasse and Südbahnhof, you sort of get the feeling of being on the Prater roller coaster.

72__The Odeon Theater
Rich and poor

It is hard to imagine that this fantastic hall in the old Vienna corn exchange dating from 1890 is supposed to have stood empty for 40 years. Even empty and theaterless, the hall seems enormous and immediately fires the imagination – above all of stage designers who create sculptures you can stage a play in. Since 1988, the hall has been used by the Serapions Ensemble, who had previously staged their theater productions for ten years in a cellar location on Wallensteinplatz. The internationally oriented ensemble of theatrical dancers is named after St. Serapion, who renounced all material (and therefore ultimately superfluous) things to live his vision of a life of true existence.

This concept of rich poverty was adopted by independent groups for the theater in the 1950s and 60s in New York, among others by the Living Theatre and the players of the legendary underground theater La Mama. The Polish theater guru Jerzy Grotowski (1933 – 1999) propagated a »poor theater« for the avant-garde of the stage in his workshops and in his theoretical writings that resulted from them. In this minimalist theater, even the actors are supposed to give up their masks, and so, comparable to Parsival's quest for the Holy Grail, advance into the Holy of Holies of theatrical art. The magic line of the original European off-theater can be traced back to, among others, the early concepts of the theater surrealist and advocate of drugs, Antonin Artaud, in Paris in the 1920s.

This disconcerting and, in its best productions, purely poetic alternative to the old, overly intellectual legitimate theater leads in a sweeping movement from Artaud, Grotowski, Peter Brook, Samuel Beckett and Pina Bausch directly to the breathlessly exciting and sometimes intoxicatingly beautiful productions of Erwin Piplits and Ulrike Kaufmann, the two leaders who alternately shape the Serapions Ensemble and together have created a theater aesthetic of their very own.

Address 2nd district, Taborstrasse 10 | **Transport** tram 2 to Gredlerstrasse | **Opening times** depend on the production, event and festival | **Tip** Do not miss seeing a production of the Hamakom Theater, 2nd district, Nestroyhof, Nestroyplatz 1, one of Vienna's most histori- cally important theater venues that has been revived only in recent years.

73___The Ost

A club like no other

The music is being played in the East. Only there are the people really prepared for everything that the coming years will bring. There is no situation in life that they are not equal to and none that they haven't had to live through. They are ready for anything. Even the past. And they have been ready for decades. Nothing can make them doubt that the present owes them a great deal. For that reason alone, the evenings in »Ost Klub (East Club)« are more wild, more colorful, more chaotic, more surreal, and, above all, more creative than anywhere else.

The lines of power in this surreal European subcontinent cross in the old »Atrium«, Vienna's first and, for a long time, only disco, directly behind Schwarzenbergplatz with its gold-glittering Soviet soldiers standing at attention high up in the air. Mysticism and absurdity bombard you incessantly until you lose consciousness: Transylvanian Roma bands appear in the harsh spotlight, Bulgarian rappers, Turkish poppers, Croatian hip-hoppers, Hasidic clarinet players, Slovenian singers. The audience is ready at any time to get excited from zero because the wild Balkan events are some of the best opportunities to keep the mainstream vampires that are lurking everywhere at night away from your throat.

A fiery crossover mix is brought onstage in the »Ost«. Break beats, blues, klezmer, dub, reggae, jazz, hardcore, trip-hop, folk, and perfectly normal abnormal dance music. The Balkan pogo and tango from the Volga.

The parties are notorious and sometimes endless. For a short time, the »Ost Klub« was called »World of Music«. That was pretty boring and sounded like a didactically orientated vinyl shop. Boring but fitting, because in the »Ost«, there is not just Eastern music but world music. That's why some evenings are thoroughly Caribbean or African, against the stream worldwide, from North to South, East to West, loud and sweaty, totally new Viennese.

Address 4th district, Schwindgasse 1 | Transport tram D, 71 to Schwindgasse | Opening times depending on event; concerts usually begin at 8pm, parties at 11pm | Tip Before things really cut loose in the »Ost«, there's at least time to catch an early movie in the nearby city cinema, 3rd district, Schwarzenbergplatz 7–8, one of Austria's best art movie houses.

74__The Perinet Cellar
The screaming of the lambs

This place with its far-reaching history has to be taken in from the outside. It can't be toured; it is closed off and with no reference to the birth of Viennese Actionism and its significance in the international and particularly in the Viennese art scene.

In this cellar was the studio of the actionist, communard, sectarian, sexual neurotic, and pederast Otto Muehl (sentenced in 1991 to prison at the age of 66 for child molestation that he and some petitioners had unsuccessfully attempted to have declared »artwork«). In June 1962, Muehl and his two buddies, Hermann Nitsch and Adolf Frohner, walled themselves in here for four days. Nitsch's famous *Blutorgelbild* was created between the »Gerümpelstrukturen (junk structures)« they put together (they had carried a lot of trash and scrap iron into the cellar). This »splatter painting« of blood, urine, paint, and feces surprisingly (in all likelihood also for the artists) became an icon of postwar art (Frohner and Nitsch were later, and independently of each other, honored for their lifework with the Grand Austrian State Prize).

When the three »unwalled« themselves out of the cellar after four excessive days, smeared, dirty, and having wet their pants for joy, they, as if having lost their senses, ripped apart a lamb (supposedly it was still alive shortly beforehand). At any rate, Viennese Actionism was born as an art form because the lamb was a symbol taken directly from Christian iconography and inspired the spirit of the interpreters.

A little later, the young Günter Brus also worked in the Perinet cellar. He first became known to a larger art public when he stood naked on the lectern in lecture hall 1 on June 7, 1968, and shat on the floor in front of a partly bewildered and amused, at any rate blackly humorous, partially highly pathological audience, while Otto Muehl had celebrated the murder of the American presidential candidate, Robert F. Kennedy, the day before in wild song.

1
Perinetgasse

Address 20th district, Perinetgasse | **Transport** bus 5A, tram 31 to Gaussplatz | **Tip**
Otto Muehl had another studio right around the corner, Obere Augartenstrasse 14A.

75__Peter's Operncafé

The glory of the divas

Presumably Peter Jansky could name the number of days that have passed since the death of The Immortal One in September 1977. He was her greatest fan, related by soul and by choice, and if you observe him when Maria Callas sings, one would like to believe that this greatest and most dramatic singer of all has been brought back to life for a moment, for the length of an aria, through his undying adoration alone.

The goddess of the opera then floats through the café and over the night sky of Riemergasse, which is located a few streets behind the state opera, and sometimes, in such moments, it would also seem far above it. Here is the place of true veneration. Maria Callas stands in the room, almost life-size in a photograph, a saint pasted on cardboard, while other singers by the hundreds hang on the walls in framed portraits, many with dedications to Vienna's greatest opera fan. That alone is worth a visit.

One is surrounded by these theatrical faces and voices, by great moments and triumphs, by never to be equaled and long since past people and times. You can catch up on these great moments in his café. Peter Jansky owns every relevant recording of every important production and knows practically everything about these recordings and their making.

Far beyond simple lexicon facts, he above all knows many anecdotes, stories, and conjectures that stretch from the beginnings of the opera 400 years ago to the current productions of the Vienna State Opera. Jansky is an ambler between the stage sets of the opera world who hasn't missed a perfect or off-pitch note in the last 30 years. He took over the former »Hartlauer« café in September, 1981. Martha Mödl, who in her time was a celebrated Wagner prima donna and who sang triumphantly under the batons of Karajan and Furtwängler, also sang for the Keeper of the Grail, Peter Jansky, at the opening of his café.

Address 1st district, Riemergasse 9 | Transport bus 1a to Riemergasse | Opening times Wed–Sat 6pm–2am, closed July, August | Tip The cake lover Maria Callas would certainly have enjoyed the excellent cakes in the »Café Diglas«, 1st district, Wollzeile 10.

76__ The Pfandl in Favoriten
With money-back guarantee

More than 300 years ago, in 1707, a pawn brokerage, the »Pfandl«, was opened under Emperor Joseph I to give the opportunity to the citizens of his empire who had come into financial difficulties to get short term credit for family silver to ensure they could survive the next ball season or, sometimes, just survive, period.

Living as far beyond one's means as possible has always been part of the urban way of life, and the constant need for fresh money, tied to being broke, insolvent, and suffering resounding bankruptcies, has made the Dorotheum an unstoppable and ongoing success story since its founding. During those three turbulent centuries, it became the biggest auction house on the European continent. Since the sale of the Dorotheum to a private consortium in 2001, the works of art handled in the main building in the 1ˢᵗ district are almost exclusively of top quality: antiques, jewelry, automobiles, and, in general, mostly things that are relatively capital intensive. For collectors and hunters of lost treasures who still must calculate their finances or count the money in their pockets, the exhibit cases in Dorotheergasse 17 are more like wishing rooms where they may only press their noses against the glass, out of desire, but also out of a lack of assets.

In Favoriten, however, in the old, lower middle class-infused workers' district, rather more modest wishes are catered to. Objects of fantastic desire and passion can be found collected in a single auction; surreal moments of happiness in the midst of a middle class environment. Things you never wanted to own and bid on just the same, pure gold amongst pure rubbish, but if you understand the true value of a totally undervalued bid – and are the only bidder to do so.

Things that do not find an enthusiast willing to bid on them are afterwards given a set and usually very attractive price and offered for sale.

Address 10th district, Erlachgasse 90 | Transport tram 6, 67, bus 7A, 14A, 65a to Wieland-platz | Opening times Mon–Fri 9am–6pm, Sat 9am–5pm | Tip The power substation in Humboldtgasse 1–5 is as architecturally distinct as the Dorotheum in Favoriten.

77__The Phil
The design for the future

»Phil« can be anything. And, in a certain way, it is. For exemple, you can drink coffee just like in a real coffeehouse, but then also buy the chair you happened to be sitting on. In addition, there are books, hot off the presses – not just newspapers as is otherwise customary. The books are just lying around, usually up front at the entrance like gifts on a traditional German Christmas gift table; a small but reasonably current selection that doesn't, however, seek to be mainstream but rather handpicked and special. The books are sealed in plastic because of the coffee and cocktails that are consumed here, but there is always a reading copy that you can take and decide, while sitting on a sofa, whether you want to own it or not. Occasionally, books are even actually purchased.

The »Phil« has something like a bar, and also sandwiches and chili con carne. The word »Phil« implies »what you like«. After all, that is the meaning of phil(e), and that is why you say it long and drawn out, as in »feel«. Now and then you can read that the »Phil« is the future of the Viennese coffeehouses, sort of a counterdesign that revises the long outdated and dust-covered maître d' structure, so that, in the short or long term, the Viennese coffeehouses will be able to survive in the future.

But in reality, the »Phil« is the design for the future of bookstores. The non-book is winning the race more and more and generates, as they say today, fat profits. Real books of paper and cardboard are quickly becoming more of a decorative accessory. And if you follow the evidence in Apple's and Google's marketing strategies, they are only going to be written for the iPad and Kindle. Also, nobody is going to need publishers anymore. Or coffeehouse waiters; so it could happen that you might have to chase after or catch a waiter head-on who is actually not a book salesman, in this bookstore so beloved by members of the Pirate political party, bobos, and seed-bomb throwers.

Address 6th district, Gumpendorfer Strasse 10–12 | **Transport** bus 57a to Getreidemarkt | **Opening times** Mon 5pm–1am, Tue–Sun 9am–1am | **Tip** »Saint Charles Apotheke« is a hybrid like the »Phil« that has existed since 1886 and, after being remodeled, is today very modern. You'll find it in Gumpendorfer Strasse 30, where occasionally exclusive evening dinners are held.

78___The Point Zero

Absolute measurement

Even the hypercritical architect and radical aesthetic Adolf Loos (1870–1933), builder of the famous bar named after him, considered St. Stephen's Cathedral to be the most beautiful and worthiest house of God in all Christendom. Especially when seen by candlelight. The Turks, during their last siege in 1683, didn't so much see the cathedral's measured and mystical numerological beauty as they did its religious and, above all, military significance. They had drawn it oversized on their maps and concentrated their (fortunately light) artillery on it.

The Viennese themselves prayed for their rescue around the clock in the cathedral and in its chapels until the relief army under the Polish king Jan Sobieski started the successful counterattack from the heights of Kahlenberg on September 12 with his heavy cavalry, the legendary Hussaria, the Polish Hussars.

The city, already on its knees, was saved, as is well-known, in its last remaining hours. It seemed like a miracle. Since that time, all roads have led to the cathedral. And so it was obvious to see »Steffl« not only as the cultural and religious mid-point of the Habsburg monarchy, but also its geographical as well. Only a few steps behind the south portal, chiseled in a plate in the ground, is point zero of the old monarchy, the so-called origin point of coordinates for cadastral measurement of Austria and its crown lands. From this point, on which you can easily put your finger or, even more easily, your foot, the whole empire was measured, in all directions – which was important in determining distances and assessing taxes and state income. Also chiseled there are the internationally legible latitudes and longitudes, whereby the longitude still refers to the Canary Island of Ferro, Europe's most western point. It wasn't until 1884 that Ferro was replaced by the observatory in Greenwich, London, as the reference point through which the zero or prime meridian now runs.

Address Stephansdom, 1st district, Stephansplatz | Transport U1, U3 to Stephansplatz | Opening times Mon–Sat 6am–10pm, Sun, hols 7am–10pm | Tip The highest point accessible to tourists in the cathedral is the Türmerstube (tower-keeper's room), 72 meters and 343 steps high.

KO.ORDINATENURSPRUNG
DER
K.K. KATASTRALVERMESSUNG
1817 – 1837
FÜR DIE KRONLÄNDER
NIEDERÖSTERREICH.
MÄHREN. SCHLESIEN
UND DALMATIEN
Geogr. Länge: 34 02' 27"32 östl. v. Ferro
Geogr. Breite : 48 12' 31"54

79__ The Porgy & Bess
This whole jazz thing!

Vienna's best jazz club is named after the opera of the same name by George Gershwin. Since 1935, Gershwin's opera has been continually and fantastically reinterpreted as if it were timeless and everlastingly valid. The endless story of love and passion is also the story of jazz. The jazz harmonies, the lonely saxophone, and the anguished drums have remained glued to the lights of the big city until this day. Jazz was always the urban rhythm needed by modern man when he was desperate and lonely, but it is also grounded in his sweaty lust for nights of excesses in bars, in ecstasy, crowded dance floors, and poorly-lit flop houses. Jazz was, before it became intellectualized, the bright red-lit underworld sound, and as if echoing jazz's own story, it is often said about »Porgy & Bess« that it was once a dirty porno movie house.

An attempt was made to reconstruct the stories of the many clubs, bars, and cabaret stages that have been in Riemergasse 11 over the last one hundred years. It was discovered that back in the 1940s, French musicians were already jamming in the cellar of the former »Rondell«, conscripted, as it were, by the music-loving occupation forces, and after the war, the two Viennese musicians Friedrich Gulda (later a famous Bach interpreter) and Joe Zawinul (who founded the legendary jazz band, Weather Report, with Wayne Shorter) jazzed together and called the place »Studio 1«.

Even if »Porgy & Bess« is very heavy on jazz, the club gives up the stage for a huge and unprejudiced crossover that features the playing of such diverse people and bands as the Johnny Winter Group, the Paul Kuhn Trio, the Nigel Kennedy Quintet, Keb' Mon and Band, or such unusual soloists as Curtis Stigers and Jack Bruce (Ex-Cream).

Young Viennese talent is also introduced in a facility called the »Strenge Kammer (severe chamber)« and strengthened for the continuation of its life in jazz.

Address 1st district, Riemergasse 11 | Transport bus 1a to Riemergasse | Opening times
Advance ticket sales Mon–Sun after 4pm; the shows usually begin around 20:30pm |
Tip Vienna's oldest jazz cellar, the very ambitious »Jazzland«, has existed since 1972 on
Franz-Josefs-Kai in the 1st district.

80___The Prückel
On the Ring

The fact that foreigners, above all the Germans, particularly love the »Café Prückel«, and that the mere mention of this distant scene of their coffeehouse happiness magically brings tears to their eyes, might just have to do with the fact that an usually large number of Viennese frequent the »Prückel«. In stark contrast to the Viennese themselves, who can hardly disguise their distaste for other Viennese, the Viennese are loved by the Germans beyond all reason – particularly the charming examples of the old Moser and Hörbiger-type characters that are occasionally still encountered in the person of yesterday's waiter or the steadfast newspaper reader, despite his disgust over the world. And the new, colorful patchwork Viennese who like to cozily style themselves as bobos, who sometimes, with kit and caboodle, and especially on Sunday, also disturb the peace in the Prückel.

The German poet Reinhold Schneider wrote his melancholy farewell to life, *Winter in Wien*, in the »Prückel« shortly before his death in 1958. A photographic portrait of him is still keeping the spot warm where he used to sit. The »Prückel« is also the setting of turbulent developments and the meeting place of lost souls in contemporary novels, which is mainly because a lot of Viennese writers spend their day here. Almost everybody visits the »Prückel«.

In other coffeehouses, they have to use cardboard buddies (as in the »Café Central«) to point out that a hundred years ago, writers of note used to visit there, revered and disdain each other, and, sometimes – to the joy of the Viennese – slapped each other's faces. In the »Prückel«, almost all of them are still there. And none of the attentive newspaper readers taking so casual and yet interested note of each person who comes and goes from behind their papers is surprised that in the course of a lucky day, nearly the whole of the Viennese literary community shows up in order to get through to the night with mélanges and small black coffees, recognized but not acknowledged, and constantly tossing greetings all about.

Address 1st district, Stubenring 24 (Dr.-Karl-Lueger-Platz) | **Transport** U3, bus 1A, tram 2 to Stubentor | **Opening times** daily from 8:30am–10pm | **Tip** In Ewald Plachutta's restaurant, across from the »Prückel« and past Dr.-Karl-Renner-Platz at Wollzeile 38, is the best and most varied beef kitchen in Vienna.

81 The Qualtinger Toilet in the Bar Wien

In the cellarmaster's cellar

Helmut Qualtinger has been conspicuous in Vienna since the 15th of November, 1961, at the latest. On that day, the Austrian TV station ORF had transmitted his »Herr Karl« directly into the living rooms of the unsuspecting Austrians. As a thoroughly begrudging stockroom clerk, he is seen whining in the cellar of a delicatessen about his boyhood and his long since missed opportunities, of which he had had a great deal as a perfidious tag-along during the Nazi period. With many television viewers feeling only indirectly addressed, yet embarrassed by it, the protest reaction was fierce. It was only after it became generally recognized that Qualtinger could possibly have meant only the others – the neighbors, the out-of-towners, or just about anybody else that more or less had happened to be among the crowd of 700,000 standing at the roadside when Hitler entered Vienna in March 1938, that the play became a success, and over the course of the years, Qualtinger became one of the city saints.

There are hardly any traces of him today, although he was at home here in this quarter and lived until his death in 1986 in Heiligenkreuzerhof behind Schönlaterngasse. He still lives in a couple of anecdotes, in anti-bourgeois stories of salvation and exorcisms (his last role was as the cellarmaster Remigio da Varagine, in Umberto Eco's *The Name of the Rose*, who was the last heretic to burn at the stake).

When you go to the toilets down in the cellar in the »Bar Wien«, you can hear his voice, consistently, at first a bit indistinct behind the heavy doors, occasionally outraged, perfidious, and self-pitying, as it was back then in the historical year of 1934/1961. You are able to enjoy him, standing, sitting, a couple of seconds of deep Viennese contemplation. An exhilarating feeling – relieving yourself while Qualtinger recites Herr Karl.

Address 1st district, Biberstrasse 8 | Transport U3, bus 1A, tram 2 to Stubentor | Opening times Mon–Sat 7pm–3am | Tip Qualtinger's regular tour of late-night bars ran, among other places, through Bäckergasse (»Oswald & Kalb«, »Kaffee Alt Wien«) to Milchgasse (»Caféclub Gutruf«).

82__The quartier21
Rebirth of the cool

Within the Museum Quarter, with the Leopold Museum, the Kunsthalle, and the mumok, is the quartier21, the cool undercurrent of artistic activities in an endless loop of creativity that, in a sense, supplies the bonus tracks to the great exhibition halls. The »21« here doesn't just abstractly stand for the 21st century but rather, in the process, also generates the contemporary art scene's password: contemporary.

The quartier21 is a fast-beat mix / remix:load / reload of different artistic and commercial forms of communication. A hairdresser's salon is as much a part of it as are the exhibition rooms for digital art, fashion, and design, the art display window that is available for use by practically any artist, as well as a comic automat, sound passages, editorial rooms, the Archive for Culture and Music, and, not least of all, a disgustingly normal photo booth, which reminds at least those who know something about artistic tradition that the surrealists Salvador Dalí and André Breton, the earliest remixers of the European avant-garde, had fun with such machines.

At present, the quartier21 consists of about 60 to 70 individual exhibitions, studios, showrooms, and shops, which, taken together, serve a relatively fresh understanding of art that has hardly any relation to the former guidelines of art.

What is staged in quartier21 are interventions against conventional understandings of art.

This doesn't make the term art more transparent, but the interconnected multi track systems of an interdisciplinarian perception create their own complex realities.

The quartier21's clean art laboratories are now already synthesizing the future (tomorrow they will inevitably be passé!). New fields of creative friction, rapidly read in codes, and creative dream machines are being fashioned that should be of interest, particularly to people who have just turned 21.

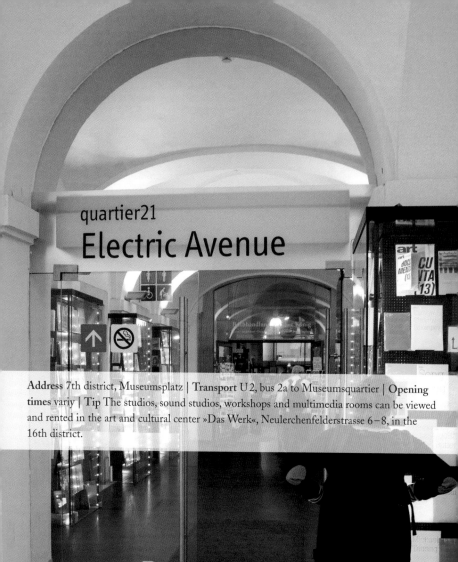

quartier21
Electric Avenue

Address 7th district, Museumsplatz | **Transport** U2, bus 2a to Museumsquartier | **Opening times** variy | **Tip** The studios, sound studios, workshops and multimedia rooms can be viewed and rented in the art and cultural center »Das Werk«, Neulerchenfelderstrasse 6–8, in the 16th district.

83__ The Rote Bar

It continues upstairs

Sometime during the evening, usually around 10pm, the curtain falls in the Volkstheater, and then, after the performance, the »Rote Bar« is opened upstairs. A fantastic, pompous, and, naturally, totally theatrical venue, bright red and as plush as the »Orient«, the luxury hourly hotel in Tiefer Graben. With a bar and a small stage, the »Rote Bar« has a touch of vaudeville, revue theater, and burlesque, but also something of agitprop and class warfare, or, simply put, a people's theater, as if the Winter Palace or the Burgtheater and the Hofburg had just been stormed. Actually, the Volkstheater was founded by free-spirited Viennese bourgeois and opened in September 1889 as a countermodel to the Burgtheater, whose productions were still imperially pompous at the time. Since then, classics are strictly staged in their respective zeitgeist, and the folk theater dramas and comedies are carried to extremes. With close to 1,000 seats, it is the largest theater in the German-speaking region.

After the official performance, everyone can »be onstage« in the »Rote Bar«. Most actors, out of natural inclination, take massive advantage of this opportunity. You experience them live, unmasked, not to be overlooked, and also not to be not heard, more exalted than earlier on the stage, relaxed and, sometimes, when they have seemingly taken leave of their senses, they impersonate or parody themselves, or do crazy things for the sheer pleasure of it. Surrounded by admirers and critics, cornered by colleagues, and encircled by their own imagination, there are unending encores in unending variations.

Naturally, the premiere celebrations are legendary. They dance on the tables and, if he is there, box with the pope.

And because the »Rote Bar« is as wonderfully disreputable as the bars used to be roundabout the Praterstern, they regularly have raunchy song nights, literary vaudeville nights, poetry slams, and tango Argentino – all right in your face.

Address 7th district, Neustiftgasse 1 | Transport U 2, U 3, tram 1, 2, D, 49, bus 2A, 48a to Volkstheater | Opening times When the performances have ended in the Volkstheater; entrance around 10pm | Tip If you prefer it airy, you should visit the Dachboden bar in the designer hotel »25hours« high above Weghuberpark (long terrace), 7th district, Lerchenfelder Strasse 1−3.

84__ The Scene of
Harry Lime's Accident

He was dead immediately, goodsir.

Everything would probably have been different if Holly Martins, the author, had actually gone to Stiftgasse 15, as he had said to the American checkpoint officer at the station. But in the best and most famous film of Vienna, *The Third Man*, by Carol Reed, which has been running in the Burgkino since its premiere in 1950, the Stiftgasse is the Josefsplatz, and number 15, in which Harry Lime is supposed to have lived and in which the caretaker, who was later murdered, was still polishing the lamps, is Palais Pallavicini, Josefsplatz 5. So many things are wrong right from the start. Also, the film's key scene is never shown; it is just described in differing versions by various witnesses with differing interests.

»Mr. Lime is dead. An accident, knocked over by a car in front of the house, have seen it myself.« Paul Hörbiger, who plays the caretaker, says these words right to the face of the shocked Joseph Cotton. And Alida Valli, Orson Welles' beautiful mistress, will say a little later, »I've wondered about it a hundred times, if it really was an accident.«

Baron Kurtz, who also is a member of Harry Lime's gang, leads Holly Martins across the street to the monument of Emperor Josef on the square of the same name and says, »He died here.« The Baron is lying through his teeth, since, as eventually comes to light, Harry Lime didn't die at the foot of Emperor Josef, but rather is shot at the end of the film by Holly Martins in the sewers of Vienna.

The third man, who helps to carry the supposedly dying Harry Lime across the street to the monument, is Harry Lime himself, the boss of Vienna's most notorious gang of smugglers.

The porter really was mistaken when he said, in best Viennese, »He was dead immediately. You don't have to worry about that.«

Address 1st district, Josefsplatz | Transport bus 2a to Habsburgergasse | Tip Josefsplatz 1, right behind the monument on the opposite side of the square, is the entrance to the Austrian National Library with its world famous Prunksaal (Grand State Hall).

85___ The Schutzhaus Zukunft

Viennese Madness

If you don't know the Schmelz, you don't know Vienna. In Europe's largest inner-city allotment garden colony (with 659 gardens), Vienna and the Viennese are, on the one hand, as promised in the city's promotional ads, indeed totally different, and on the other hand, totally themselves. Up here on the Schmelz, miles away from the floor wax-slick Hofburg, the wannabe in crowd with their pompously affected behavior, and the whole grand horse-drawn coach bliss of the inner city, the Viennese breathe easy and put their well-fed bodies along with their giant crispy brown pig's knuckles, on display.

The portions are simply humongous. You can't believe you ate the whole thing even if you already have a hundred times. The »Schutzhaus Zukunft«, the shelter house that is both the heart and the belly of the Schmelz, is like a biotope and oxygen tent that revives the last authentic Viennese: from late afternoon through the evening and deep into the night. They stuff away a lot and wish everyone in reach only the best, above all a healthy thirst and an even better appetite.

But what everyone really likes to do is sing. And when, in the spirit of the immortal composer and singer Pepi Kaderka, to whose memory a whole *stüberl*, the room the British charmingly call a »snuggery«, in the »Schutzhaus« is dedicated, they all chime in on a *Weanerliad* (a Viennese song) that can be heard all the way to the top of the Steinhof, you know that Vienna is a long way from being lost. Up until the second siege by the Ottoman Turks in 1683, there was a so-called *schmelzhaus*, a smelting house for the processing of iron ore up here that gave the area its name.

You don't often experience a really cozy feeling in life like the one here on the Schmelz, but it is still there, and when most of those singing along under the beautiful and almost 100-year old chestnut trees are a little sloshed, then you know that the coming generation will eventually come along, like you did, and the Schmelz will always be and has remained the Schmelz since the colony was opened in 1920.

KLEING ÄRTENVEREIN ZUKUNFT AUF DER SCHMELZ
GEGR 19... GEW 1987

SCHUTZHAUS
"Zukunft auf der Schmelz"

Ottakringer   Ottakringer

Ganztägig warme Küche | **Pächter: Bruckner & Böhm GmbH**

Address 15th district, Auf der Schmelz | **Transport** bus 10A, 12a to Auf der Schmelz; line 9 to Friedrich-Hundertwasser-Platz | **Opening times** daily 9am–11pm | **Tip** The Meiselmarkt on the Schmelz, Meiselgasse 20, is Vienna's only roofed delicatessen market (housed in a former water tank).

86__ The Sperl
With a golden fringe

Whoever raves about Vienna usually raves about its coffeehouses. Life in Vienna is defined by them more than by anything else. Goingtothecoffeehouse, sittinginthecoffeehouse, beingseeninthecoffeehouse are quintessential Viennese activities. Therefore, everybody in Vienna has his regular café (and a couple of favorite cafés to boot) where everybody knows him by name and he spends most of his public life. People coming to Vienna usually immediately copy this contemplative style of image cultivation, and that is why the city has been ranking at the number one spot unchallenged for years in the worldwide ranking of »cities with the highest quality of life«. Cities without coffeehouses are terrible failure.

All the same, the Viennese coffeehouse has been disappearing for about a hundred years. Only their immense numbers have been able to compensate for their losses. Mythical, anecdotal establishments, in which history was written and culture made, no longer exist, like the »Bristol«, »Dobner«, »Herrenhof«, »Hugelmann«, »Monopol«, »Parsifal«, »Paulanerhof«, »Pucher«, »Rebhuhn«, or the »Weghuber«, and all that remains of others, like the cafés »Central«, »Griensteidl«, and »Museum«, are their names and postcard mementos.

Only »Café Sperl«, which was opened in 1880, has hardly changed. It isn't completely authentic, but almost. Part of an authentic coffeehouse is, naturally, the waiters formally dressed in black. There was a time that the »Sperl« had them. Today, however, the guests are served by ladies dressed in white, who are sometimes summoned by the more elderly patrons with »Fräulein«. They wear white aprons and ankle-supporting sandals because they have to do too much walking in their lives. The classic sitting cashier here is, however, sometimes a man. That is confusing. But otherwise, everything is as it was: high rooms with chandeliers and plush, patinated furniture, large mirrors, billiard tables, and hardwood floors. »Sperl« is completely and down to the last detail under heritage protection.

Address 6th district, Gumpendorfer Strasse 11 | **Transport** bus 57a to Laimgrubergasse |
Opening times Mon–Sat 7am–11pm, Sun 11am–8pm, Jul, Aug, closed Sun | **Tip** The
oldest *Gasthaus* on Naschmarkt (go down Girardigasse in front of the »Sperl«) is the
»Eiserne Zeit« that has been in existence since 1916 at Stand 316.

87__ The Sperlhof

As long as man lives, he will play

In Vienna, it is mostly the waiters who serve food for thought, seldom the coffeehouses. That is because coffeehouses are sovereign beyond question: some with better and some with worse upholstery, some with superficially interesting and some with profoundly uninteresting customers, some well ventilated, and some not so well. It used to be that the number of national and, above all, international newspapers set out was the culturally relevant measure of a coffeehouse, as was the number of writers present – sometimes even the coffee itself.

For one thing, however, the often pitifully thin brews from bulk roastings have long since lowered expectations, and now, since WiFi, classic newspapers printed on paper tend to be romantic possibilities to hide an intelligent head behind them. And coffee house men of letters are something else again altogether.

Everything is different in the »Café Sperlhof«. There is only one waiter, who is also the operator and owner, the charming Herr Sommer. A friendly fellow from Leopoldstadt, who, in addition, is the barista, game maker, and a direct – well, at least an ideal – descendent of Sigmund Freud, who, as we all know, lent his ear to all comers. Stacked up high in his café are award-winning and famous parlor games, classics like »Trivial Pursuit« and »Monopoly«, but also flashes-in-the-pan with names like »Crazy Race« or »Star of Africa«. Between and behind the towering stacks of game boxes sit serious and sometimes affronted losers and happily excited, sometimes shamelessly grinning winners, usually grown-ups after work, for whom the little counter with chocolates and sweets is intended. There are supposedly more than 500 games here, and the »Sperlhof« is the only coffeehouse in Vienna, perhaps even in the known world, where you can play table tennis.

Another special feature is that Herr Sommer still accepts pre-euro schillings as payment.

Address 2nd district, Grosse Sperlgasse 41 | Transport bus 5a to Malzgasse; bus 80a to Taborstrasse | Opening times daily 4pm–1am | Tip One of the best of the modern pubs (*beisls*) in Leopoldstadt is the »Schöne Perle«, Grosse Pfarrgasse 2.

88__ The Stairway of Books
Living to read

The traffic roars incessantly back and forth. Supposedly an estimated 100,000 vehicles daily, from north to south and back along the heritage-protected transit rail route designed by Vienna's main architect, Otto Wagner. The trams squeal on the tracks, frenzied drivers ring their bells agitatedly, blow-hards and know-it-alls honk like crazy, particularly fiercely when driving off. On muggy and rainy days, some people seem to lose their minds.

From up above, from the open-air stairway of the main library, you can look at the obtrusive traffic down below and at the tent-like roof that stretches over Urban Loritz Platz like a sail. Between the two streams of traffic on the ring roads, there are interested and amused sausage eaters, kebab enthusiasts, the aimless, those waiting and pigeon watchers. Fast food stands in the hectic life at the terminal loops of lines 6 and 18.

It is a place where one could write expressionist big city poems, even though it would be a with a hundred years' delay. In praise of asphalt with an enthusiasm for machinery and motion as pure poetry. Perhaps that is why this building by the architect Ernst Mayr is compared with the villa of the novelist Curzio Malaparte on Capri.

Almost 100 steps lead up Vienna's largest open-air stairway at the south side of the main library. A lot of room for reading and for parallel worlds of books, because below the stairway is a place for thick books, epics from Vienna and the surrounding world. There are supposed to be close to 300,000 books a year in circulation, like the traffic on the ring roads. You can look south, over the steps and the tent roof, across the city to the Wienerberg. You have to love Vienna just for this occasionally flabbergasting ring junction at Urban Loritz Platz, which is also a place of metropolitan contemplation!

Address 7th district, Urban Loritz Platz 2a | **Transport** U 6, tram 6, 9, 18, 49, bus N6, N49, N64 to Urban-Loritz-Platz | **Tip** The billiards café of the multiple national champion in carom billiards, Heinrich Weingartner, is only a short walk away at Goldschlagstrasse 6.

89__The Stand-up Bar in the Schwarzes Kameel

The gentle smile in another's ear

The »Schwarzes Kameel« is so old that they are always up-to-date there. It was opened in 1618 as a spice shop by Herr Cameel, whose extensive family can also take credit for introducing the camellia, which was named after them, to Europe. In the course of the centuries, the »Kameel« was built up into one of Vienna's most respected delicatessens with the status of purveyors to the imperial court and with the later republican honor of catering state visits, after the monarchy's banquets feasts came to an end. It is a widespread rumor that the bakery rolls that John F. Kennedy and Nikita Khrushchev ate during the historic visit in Vienna in 1961 were supplied by the »Schwarzes Kameel«.

Since the 19th century, the important people and uncrowned kings and heiress apparents of the Inner City have been meeting in the »Kameel's« *Weinstube*, the forerunner of today's stand-up bar. By just standing around drinking wine and munching sandwiches, it was possible to immediately hack into the attitudes and interests in Vienna, and if you could separate the wheat from the *schmäh*, you knew after a couple of rolls with luncheon meat what was really important.

Of course, that didn't work with just one visit, but being a regular gave you an information advantage that is much more deeply anchored in the foundations of Vienna than the superficial newspaper news available to the common man. Until a few years ago, the Magic Line of Inner City rumor distribution is said to have run from »Oswald & Kalb« (Bäckerstrasse 14) to the »Café Gutruf« (Milchgasse 1), ending in the »Schwarzes Kameel«.

But besides the many words, suspicions, and certainties, the offerings named »tidbits« here are usually the reason people go there. Right next to the stand-up bar is the »Kameel Restaurant«, which has been among the most dependable in Vienna for many years.

Address 1st district, Bognergasse 5 | Transport U1, U3 to Stephansplatz; bus 2a to Bognergasse | Opening times Mon–Sat 9am–midnight | Tip Not as much *schmäh*, but equally good rolls can be had at »Trzesniewski«, Dorotheergasse 1.

90_ The Szazi

The hat legend

Just one step, and you're in another time. Naturally, you first have to come from Mariahilfer Strasse, pass through the stairwell, across a small courtyard, and go up a few steps. Then you are in a world you had thought was long since past. Wood and cast iron moulds, felt cones or stumps, a steaming bell and ancient sewing machines, liquid shellac, sandpaper and brushes, an oversized hat press and, between it all, the conformateur, an almost frightening wooden contraption that is pressed onto the head to take measurements by punching the head shape into the inserted paper with fine needles. Each head is different, says Herr Shapira; some are lopsided and asymmetrical, high or flat, wide or narrow – the way heads and people just are, usually with personality, sometimes without. People who don't think they can wear a hat possibly haven't thought it through. After all, the hat completes the man.

People who buy hats from the rack are likely doing themselves a disservice and underestimate what they are setting the hat on. A hat, in its most simple meaning, is protection; in its highest meaning, it completes its wearer and puts the finishing touch to top off his personality.

The workshop if full of finished hats; wonderful, finely crafted pieces as if one were living in more elegant times. »Szazi« has been around since 1858, and in these last 160 years, he is now the fifth hatter who has worked with these old tools in these old rooms. Everything he does, he does by hand, even the storm button on the hatband. A tiny detail that most hat makers don't consider; after all, there are more important things in life. But it is a sign of the ethic that a hat demands, and which, he says, he owes to himself and his customers.

In his almost silent humility, Herr Shapira says that he makes the best hats in the world. At least he doesn't know of anyone who makes a better one.

Address 7th district, Mariahilfer Strasse 4 | Transport U2 to Museumsquartier; bus 2a to Königsklostergasse | Opening times Mon–Wed 10am–6pm, Thu, Fri 10am–12:30pm and by appointment | Tip Wilhem Jungmann & Neffe, 1st district, Albertinaplatz 3, has the suits, jackets, accessories, and the finest fabrics to go with the hats from »Szazi«.

91_ The Tanzcafé Jenseits

All through the night

Jenseits means the hereafter, and the name alone has something excitingly morbid about it. After all, anyone who reflects about silvery moon-lit nights knows that Eros and death somehow go together. Also for high school and college students. You can only get real kicks by breaking the boundaries. The Tanzcafé was supposedly once, in its first life, a real clip joint with »hostesses«, women in genuine nylon hose and reeking heavily of sultry perfume. Even today, you can imagine the traveling salesmen and family men seeking escape, who were led liquored up onto the slippery ice of the dance floor.

The red-dominated interior has been maintained almost in its original form with minimal changes, and dates back to somewhere between the 1950s and the early 80s. And since the old genie in the bottle of wicked nights full of sweet whisperings still wafts over the cocktails and beer bottles like the fog in the head on the morning after, the »Jenseits« again enjoys the enviable reputation of being one of the best and most consequential pick-up bars in Vienna. But only after midnight. Beforehand, things are more friendly and sedate. A couple of lonely young drinkers are checking out what to do, and some barflies with a head start in getting drunk are philosophizing about life and the right way to handle women. The waiters, too, have experienced their adventures, and generously supply the people at the bar with anecdotes about nightlife. You need endurance. That's their secret.

The verbal warming up for the night is always intensified when the blue light next to the door signals that someone is coming, perhaps someone somebody's been expecting. Who fits the prey profile, and who doesn't? Sometimes whole groups come through the door already moving to the music in their heads, and are instantly and lastingly bombarded with sound by the attentive DJ. Unfortunately, an unspeakable plate of glass now separates the dance floor from the bar room, which naturally interrupts the uncomplicated flow that there used to be here.

Address 6th district, Nelkengasse 3 | Transport U3, bus 13A, 14a to Neubaugasse |
Opening times Mon 8pm–2am, Tue–Sat 9pm–4am | Tip When other clubs close,
»Goodmann« opens; daily from 3am, 4th district, Rechte Wienzeile 23.

92 ___ The Tegetthoff Memorial

Austria rules the Sea!

Larger than life, looking out over Praterstrasse toward St. Stephan's Cathedral from a height of 16 meters, stands Admiral Wilhelm von Tegetthoff, the hero of Helgoland and Lissa. He is the last great and striking reminder of a time when the Austrian fleet still sailed with and against the world's winds, and an Austrian warship, the SMS Novara (the first street left from Praterstern in the direction of the Inner City is named after it), sailed around the world.

The fact that Austrian ships sailed the world's oceans and occasionally reshuffled the cards, at least in the Adriatic, is only surprising at first glance. Austria had maintained its own Mediterranean fleet since as early as 1725, and the Habsburgs had had, since the 14th century, access to the sea in Trieste, although they had not used it militarily.

Wilhelm von Tegetthoff engaged a Danish naval squadron off the coast of Helgoland with his ships, the SMS Schwarzenberg and the SMS Radetzky, in the German-Danish War in May 1864, and thus protected Austria's ally, Prussia, which was not a strong naval power.

Although his ship was shot into flames after a short encounter and he was forced to withdraw to neutral British waters, Tegetthoff was celebrated as a naval hero and, at times, as the victor, and was promoted to Rear Admiral.

Two years later he demonstrated on the Italian fleet what he would have done, had his ship still been capable of battle. On July 20, 1866 (a day that is celebrated today by the Danube fleet annually under the Reichsbrücke bridge), Tegetthoff sank the Italian flagship »Re d'Italia« in the battle of Lissa. Tegetthoff sailed his fleet (21 ships with a crew of 7,800 men, 5,000 of them Croatian) at full speed between the Italian ships, took them under fire at close proximity, and, without regard to his own losses, rammed the Italian flagship, which sank immediately.

Address 2nd district, Praterstern | Transport U1, U2, tram O, 5, bus 80A, 82A, rapid transit S1, S2, S3, S7 to Praterstern/Wien Nord train station | Tip Directly across from the monument is the freshly renovated »Gasthaus Hansy« offering traditional Viennese cuisine as it probably tasted back in Tegetthoff's day, 2nd district, Heinestrasse 42.

93__ Thomas Bernhard's Grave

Hidden right out in the open

Whether Thomas Bernhard really hated all the Viennese like he hated their coffeehouses, their pastries, their newspapers, their weather, their Steinhof, their opera ball, and their Heldenplatz is a moot point. Perhaps he even loved them, secretly and all to himself.

People only got really upset over Bernhard at the start of his theatrical career; then they quickly became accustomed to his wild outbreaks of name-calling in his plays, his grouchy accusations, and his fatal tendency to say everything at least three times, and over and over again. Even the Burgtheater audience was delighted with Bernhard and his buddy Claus Peymann, the stage director and intendant (general director) of the Burg who so astutely staged Bernhard's plays. The audience didn't show it openly and dutifully booed to make Bernhard happy, since he only felt really comfortable and totally validated when booed and whistled off the stage. But it was his nature not to want to forgive them for the barrage of catcalls and the subsequent abuse by the press, and so, once in a while, he didn't allow his plays to be performed anywhere in Austria.

Whether he hated them or only took note of them and scorned them – he in no way wanted Viennese at his funeral, and had his death kept secret until after he was buried. Then, however, it was quickly made public that Thomas Bernhard lies buried in Grinzing, group 21, row 6, united in the grave with Hedwig Stavianicek, his »life person«, and her husband, Franz.

The beautiful wrought-iron cross' epitaph is usually closed. It can be opened by using the iron pin below the epitaph, and the names of the three united in death becomes visible. And so that under no circumstances people don't overlook Bernhard in the Grinzing cemetery, there is also an additional ivy-covered copper plate with his name at the foot of the grave.

Address 19th district, Grinzing cemetery, group 21, row 6, number 1 | Transport tram 38 to An den langen Lüssen | Opening times Nov 3–Feb, 8am–5pm, Mar 7am–6pm, Apr 7am–7pm, May–Aug 7am–8pm, Sept. 7am–7pm, Oct–Nov 2, 7am–6pm | Tip In the vicinity of Bernhard also lies the Viennese writer Heimito von Doderer (1896–1966; *Die Strudlhofstiege*), group 10, row 2, number 1.

94__ The Toboggan
The old devil's slide

Is the Wurstlprater really only a shadow of its former self, as nostalgic Prater old-timers, who knew it a lifetime ago, like to claim? At any rate, it has become very modern, brightly colored, loud, and a bit obtrusive, like every other carnival, and, in its current plasticized incarnation, as appealing as silicon breasts. So really not all that bad. Nobody seems to have known the old, and therefore authentic, Wurstlprater at any rate. People who were children in the 1960s, complain about the new Prater. And they remember, looking way back, the nostalgic wailings of their parents when they spoke of the older, at least halfway real but no longer really authentic Prater, the one of the 1930s when the Ferris wheel still had all its gondolas (today it only has half of them). Not to mention the former great Prater attractions of even earlier decades, the roller coaster (burned down in 1944), the »Big Chinaman« (a steam carousel), the gigantic concert cafés, and the many canals when half of the Wurstlprater looked like Venice.

Along with the Ferris wheel (opened in 1897), the Toboggan is one of the oldest attractions in the Wurstlprater. People have been careening down from a height of 25 meters along a 100 meter-long, spiraling slide here since 1913, making it actually the oldest wooden slide in the world.

Admittedly, it did also burn down to its trestle stumps in the Second World War and was rebuilt in 1947, along with the equally charred Ferris wheel.

The pleasure of sliding down the Toboggan is so pitifully harmless that you have to tell yourself some really scary stories to get some real excitement into it. For example about the woman who was sliding down too recklessly and was properly skewered by a meter-long splinter. And the unruly 12 year-old scoundrel who suffered a similar fate. His parents were waiting below …

Address 2nd district, Prater Parzelle 83a | Transport U1, U2, tram O, 5, bus 80A, rapid transit S1, S2, S3, S7 to Praterstern/Wien Nord train station | Opening times dependent on the weather, daily 10am–1am | Tip The Pratermuseum in the planetarium, right at the Ferris wheel, tells the story of the amusement park in many wonderful and historic exhibits.

95__ Trotsky's Garden

Here's to your health, comrades!

Supposedly, the garden used to be a lot nicer. That was before the Margaritensteg was built. This ultramodern bridge is an itsy-bitsy part of the 13 kilometers-long »Radweg Wiental« bicycle path and closes the formerly incomplete bikeway connection between the outskirts of the city in the West to the city center.

Now it cuts off the café's garden from the subway route, forcing the pedestrians and cyclists across the ramp. As a result, the view of the Wienzeile opposite is altered, which used to have a wonderfully urban touch: contrasts everywhere, noise and speed, iron, abysses, and beautiful façades. Paul Virilio, the French philosopher of speed, could have written his essays, The *Aesthetics of Disappearance* and *Polar Inertia,* in the garden of the Rüdigerhof. There is no evidence that he was ever here, but Café Rüdigerhof and its lovely sidewalk garden have always had prominent visitors.

Leo Trotsky, Lenin's great antagonist and former organizer of the Red Army, is said to have had discussions here prior to the October Revolution with Nikolai Bucharin, later chairman of the Communist International, and Josef Stalin, the subsequent dictator. The garden was the favorite place of many communists, socialists, and designers of better worlds who were guests in the nearby *Vorwärts-Haus* (see tip page 89) of the Social Democratic Party of Austria.

Even if the current guests are not as historically significant as those a century ago, most of them are interesting and prominent in the 5th district.

If you are sitting there for the first time, you'll probably admire the ornamentation, the beautiful proportions and the gilded script on the house's façade. Like the Rüdigerhof built in 1902, they are the work of the architect Oskar Marmorek. Marmorek died in 1909, a death probably only imaginable in Sigmund Freud's Vienna: he shot himself on the grave of his father.

Address 5th district, Hamburgerstrasse 20 | **Transport** U 4, bus 13A, 14a to Pilgramgasse | **Opening times** daily from 9am–2pm | **Tip** The revolutionaries who played chess in the Rüdigerhof also visited the *Vorwärts-Haus*, Rechte Wienzeile 97. The main wing of the house exists today and houses the »Archive of the Austrian Workers' Movement«.

96__The Ubl

Nostalgia, Viennese style

In Vienna, every past still has its inexorable present. Nothing really goes away, everything stays – at least as a warmhearted memory, as an idea of the fantasy, or as a pure ideal, and sometimes only as a shadow of its former self. In the luckiest of cases, however, it stays the way it always was. The »Gasthaus Ubl« appears to be such a place.

The characters in Ödön von Horváth's *Tales from the Vienna Woods* could have eaten lunch or dinner here, and it isn't hard to imagine the girls from the suburbs, the butchers, the tobacconists, the market stall owners, the traveling salesmen, cavalry captains, the barons, and the retirees from another time in this almost puristically furnished and wood-paneled *beisl*.

The *Gasthaus* could be a stage or a film set and probably has been, because the »Ubl« is so mundanely unspectacular and authentic that it almost seems a sensation in an ever-changing city.

In its prosaic simplicity, it is one of the most beautiful restaurants in Vienna. There's an old bar and a coal oven that still works, checkered table cloths, clothes hooks on the wall, and a sign identifying one of the tables as a *Stammtisch*, a table reserved for regulars. Roses bloom in the garden outside in the early summer, and you remember that there is also a *Zauberkönig*, a King of Magic, in Horváth's play.

Naturally, the »Ubl« wasn't always this way. Although it is hard to imagine today, a couple of years ago it was a pretty rundown and grungy place, a murky, dreadful *beisl*. It was dismantled by the present owners, who are staunch traditionalists, and they reconstructed it the way it perhaps once was in its youth. It is today the increasingly rare essence of a Vienna *beisl*, and that is why you will find here only original Viennese cooking, apart from the very few concessions to Mediterranean culinary fashions.

Address 4th district, Pressgasse 26 | **Transport** bus 59a to Pressgasse | **Opening times** Wed–Sun 11am–2pm and 6pm–midnight | **Tip** The museum of the legendary Viennese film classic *The Third Man* is housed in number 25.

97__The Ungargassenland

Time: today, place: Vienna

Ungargassenland is located in the 3rd district. It is easy to find even though it is not explicitly identified. The writer Ingeborg Bachmann invented it, or rather felt it, and it is as real as the reality reflected in her novel *Malina* dating from 1971. »Actually, there is only a street there.«

This strange land of self-discovery and self-denial is not, however, limited to the street Ungargasse. The land around it is located between Heumarkt and Landstrasser Hauptstrasse, including Beatrixgasse and Rasumofskygasse.

Ingeborg Bachmann lived in Vienna from 1946 to 1953, at first in a room in the Winkler's apartment in Beatrixgasse 26/I, later in number 3 and in Gottfried-Keller-Gasse 13.

For her, the images that she projected onto this quarter in many pictures and words were existential. »My Ungargassenland, which I must hold, fortify, my only land, which I must secure, which I defend, for which I tremble, for which I fight, for which I am ready to die, I hold it with my mortal hands.« So she experienced the rather sedate and, in the postwar years, quite tranquil district very dramatically.

This is where the narrator lived in Bachmann's biographical locations and mirror-image sentences, and her married lover, Ivan, and her male alter ego, Malina; Ivan in the house on Ungargasse »with the number 9 and the two bronze lions at the gate«, and the narrator in number 6.

After half a century, a lot of what Bachmann describes and invokes has of course disappeared, other things are marked with a commemorative plaque, like the house she lived in – just like the houses of other writers in the 3rd district, including Ida Pfeiffer, Karl Kraus, Robert Musil, and Jura Soyfer. The Ungargassenland *beisl*, »Zum Alten Heller« (Ungargasse 34) also remains, which Bachmann and her protagonists frequented in the book and in real life.

Address 3rd district, between Heumarkt and Landstrasser Hauptstrasse, in the western part around Ungargasse | **Transport** U3, bus 4A, 74a to Rochusmarkt; bus 4A, tram O to Ungargasse/Neulinggasse | **Tip** »Café am Heumarkt«, 3rd district, Heumarkt 15, is also a remnant of Bachmann's early days in Vienna.

98__ VALIE EXPORT's Cube
Behind glass

It was conceived as a »transparent space« by the Viennese media performance artist VALIE EXPORT and opened on the occasion of
the City of Vienna's »Women's Bureau's« event »Make Women Visible« in 2001. The structure is a cube composed solely of glass that is
installed under the railway arches between the two Gürtel roads. Under optimal lighting conditions, the cube seems to be absolutely
transparent; you can look right through it. Even in normal daylight,
it can hardly be seen. The light that is reflected by passing cars and
refracted in its glass plates alone marks the approximate differentia-
tion between its exterior and a possible interior.

Since its restoration in 2009, the »Kubus EXPORT« has been
used as a space for performances and installations made available
equally to both male and female artists, having completely distanced
itself from what was formerly presumed to be »feminist views«. Perhaps musician will be sitting there, or someone will be pacing back
and forth as if in a cage. Passersby who aren't going anywhere look
from the inside out and, separated by the bullet-proof glass, are
looked at by other passersby. Temporary residences of a house of glass,
denizens of the big city on display, performance artists, dancers, and
poets appear behind glass and light, somehow always out of place, at
random and yet so disconcerting that you can look through it, but not
away from it. The glass space is also used for panel discussions and
district-planned events relating to the Gürtel, which has made it, totally unintentionally/intentionally, into a »social sculpture«. Because
of its artistic definition, you can never be sure whether what takes
place in the »Kubus EXPORT« is art or not.

One of VALIE EXPORT's most famous and provocative performances was the »TAPP und TASTKINO (Tap and Touch Cinema)« of 1968. Passersby were allowed to reach into a cardboard box
that she wore over her naked breasts for exactly twelve seconds and
gain an insight into their blind, or at least dark, voyeuristic needs.

Address 8th district, Lerchenfelder Gürtel / Stadtbahnbogen 43 | Transport U 6, tram 2, 33 to Josefstädter Strasse | Opening times depend on the exhibition or performance | Tip The »Prinz Ferdinand« restaurant, Bennoplatz 2, not only has a beautiful beer garden, it is also one of the most beautiful and best inns in the 8th district.

99__The Vergaser Sign
A different kind of memorial

Large and conspicuous, reaching the top of the first floor, at the place where Czerningasse makes a slight bend, straightforward and objective, perfectly legible from both sides, it says *Vergaser*. It's the German word for carburetor, and you'll probably find signs saying the same thing in every other district indicating that you can buy carburetors somewhere in the back. Carburetors are components of an internal combustion engine. That is what is meant here as well, but the street's and Leopoldstadt's particular circumstances make something unintentional of the sign: a unique and almost conceptual memorial consisting of a single word, written from top to bottom, black on white, clear and without emotion, like a place marker, because *Vergaser* could also mean something – or someone – that gasses things – or people.

A couple of meters further on in the direction of Czerninplatz, there is a plaque commemorating the physician and psychotherapist Alfred Adler (1870–1937), founder of the school of individual psychology, who lived and practiced here for a time in the house at Czerningasse 7. He emigrated just in time to the USA and didn't wait in vain for better and, above all, more humane times like so many others. In the same house, 70 people were temporarily housed in so-called collection apartments, of whom only six survived their deportation to Auschwitz, Maly Trostinec, and Riga.

The neurologist and psychiatrist Viktor Emil Frankl (1905–1997) remained living in the house he was born in, number 6, across from Adler's house, until 1942. There is a plaque commemorating him as well. He was then deported to Theresienstadt, later to Auschwitz and Dachau. Frankl survived and, after being liberated from the concentration camp, returned to Vienna. His father and his first wife, Tilly Grosser, were murdered in the camp; his mother was gassed in the Auschwitz extermination camp, as were 111 other residents of this house. Almost one third of all of Vienna's Jews, about 60,000, lived in Leopoldstadt in 1938. In April 1945, there were only about 500.

dress 2nd district, Czerningasse 7 | Transport U1 to Nestroyplatz | Tip Czerninplatz
s one of the popular meeting places of the underground resistance groups during the
azi period because of its many escape routes.

100__ The Vienna Museum

Everything you need to know

Vienna reveals itself. Stories and anecdotes are told here as in no other museum in the city: a museum of self-reflection and analysis of its urban mental state, as if it had been Sigmund Freud's idea to put the city on its sometimes hard, occasionally very softly upholstered couch and let it talk on and on about dreams and realities, desires and fears, hopes and disappointments.

The life of Vienna is retold in this fabulous museum from ever-changing perspectives and from unfamiliar standpoints. Vienna's secrets are revealed and new ones created; a breathless diversity in the constantly changing light of a city that despite a certain and long-cultivatedtendency to take things easily has been repeatedly reinventing itself for some years now.

You can listen to these changes in the Vienna Museum, the heartbeat of the city and its whispering sounds, its light melodies and its tragic songs.

The makers of the exhibits make Vienna talk: about the global star Gustav Klimt, whose largest collection of paintings and objects it possesses, and about street battles and *beisl* bliss, about Vienna below ground and Vienna on the heights, Vienna all in socialist red and Vienna all in Nazi brown. After everything has been told, the city becomes legible – in outstanding publications that summarize in standard works Vienna's landmarks and path lines, the undeterminable workings of the Viennese psyche, and the complexity of its urbane present.

The Vienna Museum not only has some 300 death masks of famous Viennese men and women, it also collects curiosities from their lives – like Empress Elisabeth's eggcup, the shrunken rayon suit of the famous performer of Amadeus, Falco, and the expired »photo identification card for foreigners« belonging to the German-Austrian cabaret performer Dirk Stermann.

The Viennese only knows himself if he knows Vienna.

Address 4th district, Karlsplatz 8 | **Transport** U 4, tram 1, 62 to Karlsplatz | **Opening times** Tue–Sun 10am–6pm | **Tip** The Vienna Library in the city hall has an archive of around 500,000 volumes on the subject of Vienna and about 1,000 bequests of notable Viennese (entrance Felderstrasse, Stiege 6).

101— The Viktor Adler Market

The voices of Vienna

Ever since Prince Metternich (1773–1859) expressed the opinion that the Balkans start behind Rennweg Street (in Vienna's Landstrasse), whole districts of Vienna have been suspected of somehow being Turkish, Croatian, Macedonian, Romanian, or Serbian. In general, there is the fear that somehow the battle for Vienna in 1683 has been lost after all, with 350-years delay, because the »Turks«, – and with that, all the other Southeastern Europeans are meant as well – are no longer standing outside Vienna like back then, but are now in Vienna. At least in every market.

The Viktor Adler Markt would be almost as colorful as the Orient if it weren't dampened by the bleak black clothing worn by many of the immigrants. Definitively everything that grows, thrives, and is needed behind Rennweg can be bought here to fill the pots with back-home cooking. A couple of stands roundabout offer breathtaking kitsch and woeful imported goods from the last remaining communist countries that are probably, in view of the dumping prices touted here, being produced there under the extreme conditions of early capitalism.

The market is named after Viktor Adler, the founder of the Austrian Social Democratic Workers' Party and first foreign minister after the end of the multi-national monarchy.

The markets in Vienna always reflect the distinctive standard of living of its customers and their philosophy of life linked to it. The prominent Naschmarkt is quite thoroughly hedonistic, saturated up to the tips of its asparagus and stray strands of saffron and accordingly luxurious; the relatively small Karmelitermarkt, whose customers were blessed by inheritance and are dyed-in-the-wool biophiliacs, has a markedly young, middle class air. The Viktor Adler Market, on the other hand, is more of a vital necessity. People who shop here have to count their pennies, and therefore the dealers are constantly underbidding each other, particularly in Erlachgasse.

Address 10th district, between Favoritenstrasse and Senefeldergasse | Transport Public transport tram 6, 67 to Quellenstrasse/Favoritenstrasse | Opening times Mon–Fri 6am–7:30pm, Sat 6am–5pm, 1st Sat in the month 6am–6pm | Tip If the gastronomy at Viktor Adler Market is too rustic: »Meixner's Gastwirtschaft« (award-winning restaurant), Buchengasse 64/corner Herndlgasse, is one of the finest places to eat in Favoriten.

102__The Volkswohnpalast

A place in the sun

It was supposed to have been bigger, even more formidable and more impressive. The two architects Hubert Gessner and Josef Bittner built eight floors in the center building instead of 16 as had been planned. Vienna's first skyscraper-like high-rise was supposed to be, as the conspicuous and greatest achievement of the Social Democratic city government, the masterpiece of »communal socialism«.

It was designed as an analog to the bourgeois and feudal architecture of other districts, but it ultimately became a rather petty-bourgeois accentuated supplement to what already existed than a socio-political alternative: the People's Residential Palace consists of almost 500 apartments, some of them tiny. Its courtyards and corridors are furnished with kitschy and some sentimental details as if back then the class struggle was already history.

Nevertheless, the municipal building project, that was completed in 1926 and named after Vienna's mayor Jakob Reumann became the prestige object on the Margaretengürtel, which was stylized as the »Ringstrasse of the Proletariat«. There are five major municipal buildings between house numbers 76 and 134; the Metzleinstaler Hof (number 90−98) is also by Gessner.

The whole pathetic impact of this residential machine is still felt today in the Ehrenhof, or Courtyard of Honor, which is in front of the center building and surrounded by the side wings. The complex gained its paramount, and also historic, importance similar to that of the Karl Marx Hof during the Civil War of February 12 to 15, 1934. The republikanische Schutzbund (Republican Protection League) had its headquarters in the Reumann Hof and at first was able to defend it under the command of Julius Deutsch, who was later a general in the Spanish Civil War. They were forced to capitulate on the evening of February 12. Deutsch was able to flee, leaving behind memories of a short but fierce battle.

BÜRGERMEISTER JAKOB REUMANN 1919 — 1923

Address 5th district, Margaretengürtel 100–110 | Transport tram 6, 18, bus 59a to Margaretengürtel / Arbeitergasse | Tip The hotel »Favorita«, 10th district, Laxenburger Strasse 8–10, was, in its beginnings, a legendary workers' home in which numerous Social Democratic party congresses were held.

HIER IM REUMANNHOF
VERTEIDIGTEN AM
12. FEBRUAR 1934
SOZIALDEMOKRATEN
DIE DEMOKRATIE
GEGEN DEN FASCHISMUS

12. FEBRUAR 1984

103__ The Weisses Haus

The nomads of happiness

Off-rooms are all the rage. Every boarded-up milk shop today is at least given close scrutiny to determine whether it could be used somehow as an off-room. Most of them can, naturally, and so off-rooms are constantly being unboarded and boarded up again. This term for cultural space outside the mainstream was originally derived from Off-Broadway and was a term used in the 1960s for the theater houses that existed (or attempted to exist) outside of profit-orientated Broadway in New York.

In the same vein, larger locations with a loft character are frequently termed off-spaces, and the automatic alternative progression of off-Broadway was off-off-Broadway, scarcely capable of surviving and gasping for funds. But ideally, off-rooms make it possible for artists, curators, and buyers to make a smooth entrance into the art scene, without risk and with almost no effort. Normally, all that remains of the off-rooms is at best warm memories of parties and a couple of Likes on Facebook.

The »Weisses Haus« is a different matter. From the outset, this off-room, initiated by the resolute Alexandra Grausam, was conceived as a kind of art association. Some 350 artists have been exhibited in around 70 group and solo shows (which could be a record for the off-scene), as well as in numerous extras and so-called satellite projects at various sites.

One of the principles (ultimately out of necessity) of an off-association is to constantly change venues because the rent, at least in attractive areas, is beyond the bounds of feasibility. They change their sites and create a network with their partners that reaches deep into Vienna's cultural activities.

The »Weisses Haus« migrated from the 7th district, where it had gotten its name from a white German Georgian house, to the 1st district and then to the 5th, eventually reaching its present location in the 4th district.

Address 4th district, Argentinierstrasse 11 | Transport tram D to Gusshausstrasse | Opening times Tue–Fri 1pm–7pm, Sat noon–5pm | Tip The iconic coffee-roasting establishment »Kaffeefabrik« (which also sells vodka) is in the immediate vicinity at Favoritenstrasse 4–6.

104_ The WestLicht
The freedom of vision

The fact that Vienna, as the old, often quoted promotional ad for the city promised, actually is different (different from other major cities, naturally), has less to do with its urbane Viennese charm. It has much more to do with personalities like Peter Coeln who do not conceal their Viennese passions, but want to live them out publicly and uninhibitedly. In 2001, he therefore founded an association to support WestLicht, while he himself, it may be assumed, does everything to support the association. He is his own main sponsor. The »Kompetenzzentrum für Fotografie« (a trendy, cultural bureaucratic word monster that doesn't begin to give an idea of the poetic masterpieces and photographic works that are on display there) has become, after more than ten and increasingly successful years, Vienna's finest address for photography. However, WestLicht is currently competing with itself through its own offshoot OstLicht in the Ankerbrotfabrik, Absberggasse 27, which shows the most important representatives of contemporary Austrian photography.

WestLicht is everything at once; an auction house for photographica, a Leica gallery, an exhibition hall, a museum, a collection, and a reference library with more 20,000 books and magazines. The rapid development of this medium in the past 100 years is exemplarily shown by some 800 rare and, in part, unique and therefore particularly significant devices, beginning with the simple light boxes of the early period, when photography was still a mystery, to the current highly complex digital cameras that are already shooting into the future.

Many of the most important photographers are represented beautifully in exhibits of their works. The excellently curated thematic exhibitions, however, are of particular interest – for example, the show on Viennese Actionism or »Magnum's First«, when it was possible to reconstruct in vintage prints the first exhibit in 1955 of the world famous Magnum photographs.

Address 7th district, Westbahnstrasse 40 | **Transport** tram 5, 49 to Kaiserstrasse/West-bahnstrasse | **Opening times** Mon–Wed, Fri–Sun, hols 11am–7pm, Thu 11am–9pm | **Tip** Rare and beautiful cameras, mainly analog, lenses, and sought-after attachments are offered by Franz Gibiser in his collectors' shop »Camera 31«, Westbahnstrasse 31.

105_ The Wooden Tower
All the way to the horizon

When the great stretches of train track were being laid during the Industrial Revolution in the 19th century, they designed gigantic train stations to fit their own image of the new era that were like cathedrals of progress – magnificent buildings, sometimes bombastic and incurably turned into kitsch, which became totally neo-Gothic in the face of all that future. Only »great train stations« could fulfill the municipal ambition of finding the most prestigious way possible of becoming part of the modern times. Vienna even had five such train station cathedrals since all roads led to Vienna in the old Austrian Empire.

Nothing is left of these train stations. They were the main targets of attack by Allied bombers in the last war. The postwar buildings have also been torn down in the meantime. The new Vienna Central Station is being built to replace the Vienna South Station. It will be Europe's largest and most modern station. The so-called Bahnorama, the information center, informs the public about its ambitions and prospects, and from the construction's tower, it can be seen how splendid it will be. This wooden tower constructed of spruce is just short of 67 meters high, and a glass elevator brings the visitor to the 40 meters high lookout platform.

It is not the most beautiful view of Vienna. Close by, Gürtel Vienna can be seen with its depressing architecture of graying façades. Somewhere down there on Wiedener Gürtel, Edip Sekovitch, the world boxing champion, was knifed, and the thought of this murder fits this Gürtel tristesse. Through the chain-link fence preventing unhappy Viennese from leaping down into the city you can see to the north all the way to Leopoldsberg and Floridsdorf, beyond Favoriten in the South and, in the West, to far-off Hitzing. Amateur photographers take aim at Vienna with their arm-long lenses, and the visitors are kindly asked to stay no longer than 15 minutes on the platform, vibrating ever so lightly under your feet.

Address 10th district, Favoritenstrasse 51 | **Transport** U1, tram O, 18, bus 13A, 69A, rapid transit S1, S2, S3, S5, S6, S9, S15 to Südtiroler Platz | **Opening times** Summer 8am–10pm, winter 8am–6pm | **Tip** There is an even better panorama view of the city from the »Le Loft« bar and restaurant on the 18th floor of the Hotel Sofitel, 2nd district, Praterstrasse 1.

106__ The Workshop of Wild Herbs

For a new culinary society!

Being uncomfortable with the middle-class synthetic culture of excess has always led to unusual exercises in escape. Affluence is just as much the mother of invention as necessity, and there is something unexpectedly liberating in taking a side step at a high level into the normally ignored leftovers of a tiny paradise. We are not lost yet is the happy message for the microwave-irradiated people of today. Instead, we are hot on the heels of nature again. Everything is suddenly so easy. You just have to close your eyes and then open your mouth to appreciate the bucolic undercurrents of life. After all, nature is everywhere, in the Vienna Woods as well as in the rambling Steinhofgründe park.

That's where Gertrude Henzl collects what grows and is edible. She doesn't sow, she harvests. The former lawyer has made a profession out of her obsession with looking on her knees for edible things. In her purist workshop, she composes in small amounts wholly unknown delicacies out of wild herbs and wild vegetables; herb salts, blossom sugar, jellies and fruit mats, vegetable candy and chutneys.

Her products are so rare, handpicked, and require so much work that you shouldn't get excited at all about the precisely calculated prices. Supermarket-coded penny pinchers have a tendency to do that. It's like a very fine wine that you can't get at discount prices, as we all know. Her whole harvest of deadnettle was barely enough to make just four bottles of her deadnettle syrup with violet sugar.

Gertrude Henzl also organizes so-called hiking seminars in her harvesting grounds that teach how to create the basis for a new pleasure awareness and an effective network of untapped sources of food. And she has a vision: at the end of all the collecting, there will be a new culinary society which will perhaps save the world.

107___The Wortschatz

Take-away

As is well known, the Viennese don't suffer from a lack of words. It comes along with the constant *schmäh*, as well as the generally prevailing ambition of wanting to get in the last word. In this respect, everybody carries their own *Wortschatz*, or vocabulary, around with them, and a trenchant formulation immediately finds admirers who adopt it and add it to their own repertoire of quick-witted repartees. In the final analysis, most Viennese are would-be writers or at least story tellers, just as the many writers in Vienna are would-be Viennese.

That is why the Viennese read more than others, not only at home but also when they go out; they read practically everywhere, and often in competition with one another. Newspapers are taken in occupation in coffeehouses, hidden under the table, and only surrendered under protest, since the Viennese are so downright obsessed with their own readerbodies (which are so important to them that they actually have a word for it). The trams often resemble rolling reading rooms, and hardly anyone sits down in a park without a book. The resources are always scarce despite a dense supply network, public libraries, excellently stocked bookstores, and a wide range of second-hand bookshops.

The »Wortschatz« was installed on Margaretenplatz to make the indulgence of the basic Viennese propensity for the word extremely convenient, even when just walking by. It functions according to a principle similar to social networking. You give and take. This is so provoking for some nighttime passersby, especially those that can't read, that they demolish the bookcase. There is a potpourri of books in the »Wortschatz« that you can take out and supplement at will with gusto. Not everything is good, but everything is a matter of taste. You'll find easy reading that will be enough for a few reading steps around the corner or from one tram station to the next. But there are also cumbersome heavyweights that have the stuff to turn your life around. Maybe that's why they were turned in.

Address 5th district, Margaretenplatz | Transport bus 12A, 13A, 59a to Margaretenplatz |
Opening times daily 24/7 | Tip You'll find good books to read that can be borrowed or
exchanged in »Silberwirt's« Gastgarten, Schlossgasse 21 (in the »Schlossquadrat« directly
on Margaretenplatz).

108_ The Xpedit Kiosk
With currywurst

It is a familiar fact that the currywurst known today around the world was invented on the 4th of September, 1949, by Herta Heuwer in her sausage stand on Kantstrasse in Berlin. Of course she didn't invent the sausage, just the sauce that turns a *Wurst* into a currywurst. Frau Heuwer had this sauce patented with the inventive name of »chillup«, which leveraged her fast-food stand up to 17 employees when the currywurst reached its zenith in Berlin. The currywurst has since been retinkered into countless unpatented variations – culinarily enhanced or trivialized. After all, all you need besides the *Wurst* is ketchup, curry powder, some chili, and cayenne pepper. The original *Wurst* is supposed to be cut with a knife and not shredded. In addition, the only proper way to eat it is standing up.

The currywurst became a symbol of the city, along with the Brandenburg Gate, barbed wire, and the *Schiessbefehl* (order to shoot). A teeny weeny part of Berlin is also thriving in Vienna on Margaretenstrasse at the corner of Schleifmühlgasse, one of the most important internationally compatible gallery locations. The original Berlin currywurst can be found in the Xpedit Kiosk – almost an affront in Vienna to the *Würstlstands* with their *Käsekrainers*, *Waldviertlers*, and *Burenwursts*. But the curry-laden sausage is also a small object of yearning, a little bit of gusto as a fiery access to the far-away and currently very hip world capital of art that still pleasantly inspires the Bohemian fantasy with its barbed wired-scratched behind. In combination with an original Berlin beer, it costs six euros, and the kiosk appears inside, in its casual improvisation, as if an admirer had dismantled it right at the intersection of Oranienstrasse and Wiener Strasse in Kreuzberg and had it faithfully rebuilt it here. Just like Berlin, the Kiosk makes a charmingly unprofessional impression; the waiting times are too long, but the place is friendly, and the toilets are smeared with epigrams and anarchistic jokes just like in the real underground.

Address 4th district, Schleifmühlgasse 7/3 | Transport bus 59a to Schleifmühlgasse | Opening times Mon–Sat 10am–midnight, Sun, hols 2pm–10pm | Tip »Gaststätte am Rilkeplatz« (a minute away by foot), although not as hip as the Kiosk, is really cozy, with a coal oven and tables full of beer-drinking buddies.

109__Yppenplatz

Summer quarters

For a couple of years now, Yppenplatz has been such an in-place that it is naturally avoided by the in-crowd and the restaurant-going avant-garde. The Brunnenmarkt, which belongs to Yppenplatz, is too established and hasn't been an inside tip that would guarantee exclusivity for a long time.

It is way too bourgeois-Bohemian, which is practically inevitable in the Vienna of people in their late thirties, but still too mundane a part of everyday life for many an urbane trailblazer. In this respect, the square is a venue that once was in and is now just established.

And so on Saturdays, and above all when the weather is good, it is hardly possible to get a sunny spot in front of a café, and it appears as if many of the newspaper-reading couples who intimately sneer together at the world beneath the headlines, and the aficionados of latte macchiato with closed eyes have taken root here.

The only time you rise up is to see or be seen better, or to dive into the rear of one of the shady cafés and restaurants to refill your brunch plate. The »de la go«, with its brilliant buffet and first-class wines, is particularly to be recommended here, especially since the waiters are among the most adept in their field.

In any case, you should get there early and leave late, in order to be able to enjoy this wonderful Viennese way of easing into the weekend while seated. As a part of an extensive street market that runs down Brunnengasse past Grundsteingasse, the square is in every respect a prime spot, with organic farmers, growers of natural wines, and occasional traveling performers who provide entertainment for an invariably interested audience. The Brunnenmarkt itself is, like many other Viennese markets, a colorful but mostly uniformly oriental matter that does have, however, some original stands where carps are still slaughtered and all kinds of creatures are carved into their individual components.

Address 16th district, Yppenplatz | Transport tram 44 to Bergsteiggasse | Tip Running down Brunnengasse is one of Vienna's last street markets, the Brunnenmarkt.

110_ The Zauberkastenmuseum

The feasibility of the illusion

Most passions are developed by the age of twelve. At least that is the case with men. Naturally, they are cultivated only later because it takes a certain expertise and intensive closeness to bring things to perfection. But their origin usually lies in this early and more or less carefree time marked by curiosity and awesome self-determination. And so it was with Manfred Klaghofer. He was given a book about magic when he was a boy, and later, a magic set. These sets of magic tricks at first seem as harmless as any other parlor game. But they are basically put together like those earlier, elaborately crafted and today very valuable sets that professional conjurers and magicians used when they appeared before constantly amazed audiences in the 19th century.

»We know that they are deceiving us, but we can't recognize how«, the Roman physician Sextus Empiricus had already noted. People love magic tricks, and whoever has mastered one likes to show it off. We want to figure it out and know how it works, to admire the illusion still more by understanding it. On the other hand, it is wonderful to suspend disbelief and just marvel at the illusion. The magician must play the role of a magician and believe, at least for a moment, in what he is doing.

Manfred Klaghofer mastered playing the role and his first set of magic tricks so expertly that he was accepted into a renowned Viennese magicians' association when he was only 15. He bedazzled his audiences on weekends in guesthouses and at parties, often on the spur of the moment. If you want to get the attention of girls at that age, you have to come up with something special one way or another.

Later on, after many years as a successful businessman, he remembered that wonderful time and began to collect magic kits on a grand scale. Today, he has the world's largest collection: more than 2,400 sets from every continent and spanning three centuries.

Address 12th district, Schönbrunner Strasse 262 | Transport bus 10a to Bischoffgasse (away from the city); line U4, bus 10A, Schönbrunn station (towards the city) | Opening times Every 1st Sun in the month 10am–4pm | Tip The »Circus and Clown Museum«, 2nd district, Ilgplatz 7/1, has a similar charm carried by the enthusiasm of its makers.

111 The Zweckentdeckungs-Salon

A matter of point of view

Upcycling is a strange word, both written and spoken, and somehow even worse than recycling, but at least more interesting. Upcycling is a term for a creative process that redefines a material or function or provides it in unexpected contexts with another identity. Upcycling is also a cultural attitude and an opportunity to pin one's own creativity on the past or proven creativity of others. Upcycling demands wittiness, and wit is an old word for intelligence. Upcycled objects, when they are good, are invariably witty. They live from the unexpected, from shifting the borderlines, and from their misuse that is sometimes the discovery of a use, which is the meaning of the salon's name in German, *Zweckentdeckung*.

The designer Tina Lehner artistically investigates this endless variety of possible uses in many of her works. For example, she makes a voluminous wooden chandelier out of old picture frames, or a transparent wire sculpture out of the wire frames of lampshades, without the shades, placed on top of each other around a single light bulb that reaches from the floor to the ceiling.

This redefining of the defined uses of everyday items makes it totally senseless to breed animals to kill for their fur. There is an overabundance of furs; everybody's rich old aunt has a closet full of them, as the pawn shops and the mothball-loaded horror chambers of bad taste do.

So anyone who wants a bearskin doesn't have to shoot one first. And doesn't have to have it sewn together by modern furriers. It can be sewn together from old mink and Persian lamb coats, as Tina Lehner has done in one of her masterpieces.

But since autonomous aesthetics wants to prove its mettle not only in the spectacular, but on a more modest scale as well, there are also useful objects (drinking cups, for example) in limited series.

Address 6th district, Gumpendorfer Strasse 63 b | **Transport** bus 13A, 14A, 57a to Haus des Meeres | **Opening times** Fri 1pm–6pm and by appointment | **Tip** Fantastically off-beat furniture by very imaginative designers can be found at »das möbel« at Gumpendorfer Strasse 11.

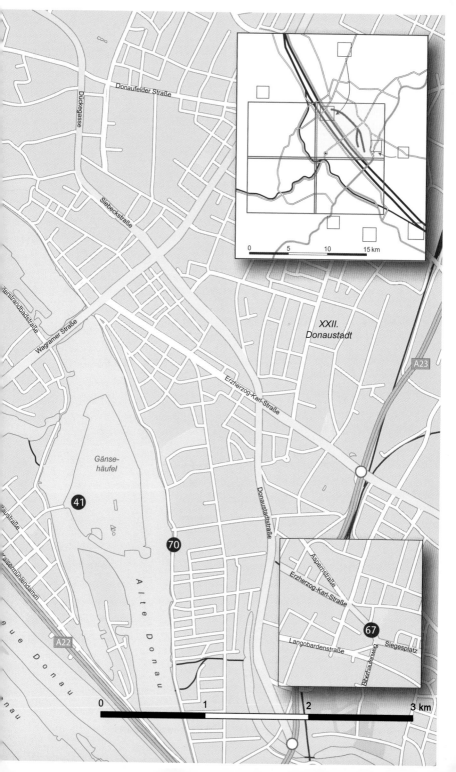

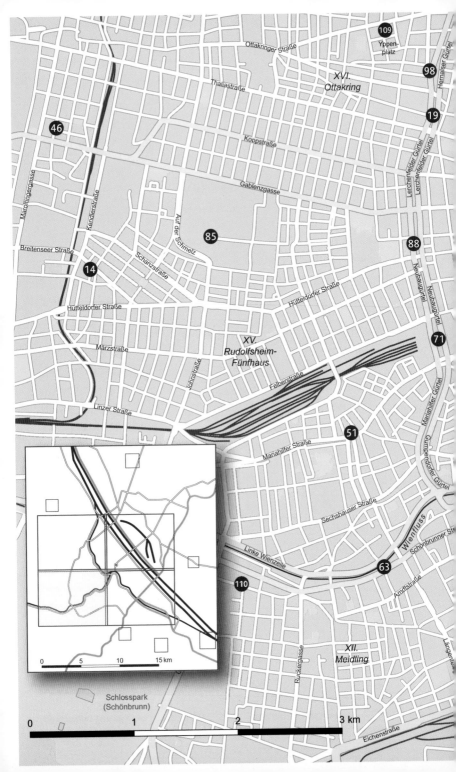